A Lower-Middle-Class Education

For Bob Knickerbocker,
without whom this + a
lot else would not have
happened. Bob Davis

A

LOWER-MIDDLE-CLASS

EDUCATION

By Robert Murray Davis

UNIVERSITY OF OKLAHOMA PRESS : NORMAN AND LONDON

Also by Robert Murray Davis

Evelyn Waugh, Writer (Norman, 1981)
Evelyn Waugh and the Forms of His Time (Washington, D.C., 1989)
Mid-Lands: A Family Album (Athens, 1992)
Playing Cowboys: Low Culture and High Art in the Western (Norman, 1992)

A version of "Healthy Boy-Girl Relationships: A Distraction" appeared in *North Dakota Quarterly* 62 (1994–95):113–126. A version of "Wise in My Generation" appeared in *texture*, no. 6 (1995), 79–83.

Library of Congress Cataloging-in-Publication Data

Davis, Robert Murray.
    A lower-middle-class education / by Robert Murray Davis.
        p.   cm.
    ISBN 0–8061–2848–8 (alk. paper)
    1. Catholic universities and colleges—United States—Case studies. 2. Small colleges—United States—Case studies. 3. Social mobility—United States—Case studies. 4. Rockhurst College—History. 5. Davis, Robert Murray. 6. College students—United States—Biography. I. Title.
    LC501.D39   1996
    378.778′411—dc20   96–4378
                                                                                                          CIP

Text design by Debora Hackworth

The paper in this book meets the guidelines for permanence and durability of the Committee on Production Guidelines for Book Longevity of the Council on Library Resources, Inc. ∞

1 2 3 4 5 6 7 8 9 10

For
Professor M. Robert Knickerbocker
Dr. James F. Scott
K.
and in memory of
Reverend Joseph A. McCallin, S.J.

We have yet to understand the thaumaturgical way in which we conceive of intellectuality.

—Lionel Trilling

I wish I had a pencil-thin moustache
So I could solve some mysteries too

—Jimmy Buffett

Contents

Contents

A Postscript and a Preface

Unless you read my book *Mid-Lands: A Family Album*, you probably don't know about me. Even then you wouldn't know much, because that book is less about me than about the experience of a place and time, the small-town Midwest in the postwar, pre-Eisenhower years. Boonville, Missouri, seemed outside time and the process of change. Most of the time in *Mid-Lands* I used "we" to speak of experience I had unconsciously shared with my contemporaries and, even less consciously, with a whole town and region.

The plural was also appropriate because the story was about my family and in the family's oral conventions. Of course, like most male autobiographies, it was really about my father, or my relationship with him. In his autobiography, Auberon Waugh used the title *Will This Do?* We ask the question when it is too late to get an answer that might be devastating.

Being Matt Davis's son and a resident of Boonville wasn't always easy, but at least it was a clearly defined role as a white Catholic heterosexual boy with minor athletic talents who seemed fairly normal except that he read too much and sometimes said odd and unaccountable things. I thought Boonville incredibly narrow and limited. Nobody seemed to have traveled much farther than Kansas City, St. Louis, and the Ozarks, and the community's intellectual and artistic interests seemed confined within even narrower boundaries. In fact the town had plenty of room for character parts, even young smart-asses; the lines weren't too complicated; and the audience, also part of the cast, was surprisingly tolerant.

But not having read *Mid-Lands* may not be a handicap. An anonymous reader who had read it was horrified by this book, misunderstanding its tone because he seemed to suffer from a severe irony deficiency. This book was a lot harder to write because it describes what happened when I tried to change scripts. Of course, everyone has to learn, by formal or informal education, how to say the right thing at the right time, or at least come close. Looking back, I'm surprised at how difficult it was.

The title of this book is an allusion and a description, not a value judgment. Wilfred Sheed, who is only a few years older than I but has a trans-Atlantic heritage and upbringing, called one of his novels *A Middle Class Education*, using a phrase that in England used to mean that someone had attended Oxford or Cambridge University. The American equivalent is the Ivy League or one of the small, selective colleges, probably but not necessarily in New England, which charge equally high tuition and admit people who have a lot of old money or, through scholarships, those who have almost none.

Essentially, a middle-class education is supposed to help you maintain status so that you can understand what your family is saying. A lower-middle-class education is supposed to help you improve your status so that your family will not understand what you are saying. After all, education, as we were reminded to the point of nausea in the early 1950s, came from the Latin *educare*, "to lead out." Perhaps it matters less where you go than that you go. Thomas Wolfe was only partly right. You can't go home again, but you can't know what home is until you leave.

Mid-Lands is about where some of us came from. This book is about how we started going somewhere else. I won't maintain that my experience was typical of my generation (called Silent by media pundits who didn't know when they were well off) though I think it has not been uncharacteristic. Just after I thought of the title, there was a minor nostalgia boom for the late 1940s and early 1950s—the television series "Brooklyn Bridge" is a good example. By the time I revised the manuscript, the craze had gone the way of "family values" and the Republican presidency, but that world still exists, somewhere between history and uncertain memory. Perhaps this book will stir some memories in those my age and amuse, even instruct, the increasing number of those younger than we.

Acknowledgments

My thanks go to Sister Una Marie, librarian, Avila College; the Reverend Joseph E. Gough, S.J., archivist, and Todd L. Reding of the Alumni Relations office, Rockhurst College; and to Beth Davis McClary, who guided me to archival materials. James F. Scott and John C. Moore of the Rockhurst class of 1955 shared memories with me and, like Alvin Greenberg, read early drafts of several chapters. M. Robert Knickerbocker made valuable suggestions about a late version. Sarah Nestor read and improved every draft. At the University of Oklahoma, the Research Council provided a grant for travel funds; the Proposal

Services Office, copying facilities; and the Department of English, printing and other administrative services.

A Lower-Middle-Class
Education

Submerged in History

In September 1951, I turned seventeen, but I didn't know I was a member of a generation. Neither, probably, did James Brown or even Ralph Nader and LeRoi Jones, all turning seventeen that year. Willie Nelson had been eighteen and eligible for the draft since April, and Harold Lloyd Jenkins, who for some reason decided to become Conway Twitty, had registered for it three days before my birthday. Joan Rivers and Joan Collins were also eighteen, but safe. Elvis Presley, sixteen since early January, was about to start his junior year of high school, but Ken Kesey wouldn't be able to get his drivers' license, if Oregon had the same requirement as Missouri that a driver be sixteen, for another two weeks. Jerry Lee Lewis's birthday was twelve days after that; he had recently returned to Ferriday, Louisiana, from Waxahachie, Texas, where he had been expelled from Southwestern Bible Institute for playing a boogie-woogie version of "My God Is Real," in time to meet the woman who would become his first wife early in 1952. Except for Jerry Lee, we were silent because we hadn't discovered anything to be noisy about—or with. Some picked up the right instruments almost immediately; others, like me, had been told by graduation speakers that the world was all before us, but we weren't sure how far it extended or how to get there.

That world might seem small and cozy now, but it looked big and intimidating to me, and in fact it was getting larger. My seventeenth birthday coincided with the first coast-to-coast television broadcast—President Truman at the conference on the peace treaty with Japan, and NBC-TV (the suffix was still necessary) announced a daring plan to begin its broadcast day at 7 A.M. rather than at 10:30. That night Nash Ambassador (a kind of automobile) was sponsoring Paul Whiteman's "TV Teen Club," which would have seemed odd had I known about it because my parents had danced to his records in the 1920s. But we didn't have a television set, nor did anyone I knew—there were only two tv stations in the whole state of Missouri (double the number of FM radio stations), so none of this mattered to me. Nor to Darryl F. Zanuck, the movie mogul, who proclaimed that television was no threat to national radio networks or to the film industry because of the poor quality of its programming.

Confidence in movies seemed well placed, even though Louis B. Mayer had just been forced out as production chief at Metro-Goldwyn-Mayer. I probably saw at least one movie a week, sometimes two, a standard fix. Of the movies playing the first week of September, I recall a surprising number. There was the standard Biblical epic, *David and Bathsheba*, with Gregory

Peck trying to look noble and horny at the same time and Susan Hayward showing enough skin to pull in the customers but not enough to bother the Production Code office. There was the obligatory musical, *Show Boat*, with Kathryn Grayson looking soft, Howard Keel looking stalwart and corseted, Ava Gardner looking even softer, and, as usual, forlorn, Marge and Gower Champion looking bouncy, and a black man, William Warfield, looking unusually dignified for a movie of that period and stealing the show with his version of "Old Man River." In *Saturday's Hero*, John Derek was a lower-class half-back on an all-white college football team who was exploited by the rich girl as well as the athletic system and cast off when he could no longer play. Women in college didn't fare any better: Jeanne Crain was exposing the horrible effects of sorority snobbery in *Take Care of My Little Girl*. *A Place in the Sun* was obviously serious, but I knew I could never attain to Elizabeth Taylor's level and wouldn't know what to do with a compliant Shelley Winters.

All of these played at the Lyric Theatre in Boonville, now a historic monument but then just the larger and better movie house in town. A block away, the Casino ran mostly B pictures, including the most recent film starring Abbott and Costello, which I may have seen even though I no longer found them very funny. Also making the rounds was a Dean Martin and Jerry Lewis film, but I never did think them funny. Burt Lancaster appeared in the hagiography, *Jim Thorpe—All American*. Robert Mitchum was back on the screen in *His Kind of Woman* after becoming the first white celebrity to be arrested for smoking marijuana, and John Wayne, at this point an actor of sorts rather than an icon, was in *Flying Leathernecks*.

In the comic strips, someone had fallen in love with a model in "Mary Worth," and Dagwood had been wakened and gone back to sleep on the couch, but everyone in "Gasoline Alley" was young. Roy Rogers had his own comic strip. Joe Palooka, the perennial white heavyweight champion, kept his strip but was being moved from a series of films to television. Annie was still little and orphaned, years away from being a Broadway star. A new strip in the old tradition of the beast fable, starring a possum named Pogo and set in a swamp, was in its first year and beginning to edge toward political satire.

I had never seen and couldn't imagine a newspaper without comic strips, but I was interested in books. The week of my birthday, many of the books on the *New York Times* best-seller list had water in them. *The Caine Mutiny* and *Kon-Tiki* were number one in fiction and nonfiction; *The Sea Around Us* was second in nonfiction and *The Cruel Sea* third in fiction (between *From Here to Eternity* and *The Catcher in the Rye*); and James Michener's *Return to Paradise*, set in the South Seas, was still appearing. Royalty (*A King's Story,* about the Duke of Windsor) and food (*The New Joy of Cooking*) were represented as usual on the nonfiction list, but suspicion and paranoia did even better: *Washington Confidential* was third, *Crime in America,* sixth; and *Communism, Democracy, and Catholic Power,* eleventh. On the fiction list, as if to balance things out, Cardinal Spellman's *The Foundling* was also eleventh. On a more exalted level, *The Portable Henry James,* not on the best-seller list but reviewed that day in the *Times,* made the Master available to the masses. Stephen Potter's *Lifemanship,* a far better guide to the world of the 1950s, was sixteenth on the nonfiction list.

At the time, I hadn't heard of any of these books, though the ripples of cultural lag later brought some of the novels to me. But I had heard and can still sing at least parts of most of the hit songs of that week. Rosemary Clooney's "Come-on-a My House" was at the top of the charts, where Italian-Americans were perhaps overrepresented by Tony Bennett ("Because of You" and a cross-over hillbilly song, "Cold, Cold Heart"), Frankie

Laine (born LoVecchio, singing "Jezebel"), Mario Lanza ("The Loveliest Night of the Year"), Vic Damone ("My Truly, Truly Fair," also sung by Guy Mitchell with Mitch Miller) and Tony Martin, who had changed his name from Alvin Morris to sound as well as look Italian ("I Get Ideas"). Frank Sinatra and Perry Como were barely in the top twenty-five. Clooney was an anomaly—most women with hits had monosyllabic last names: Dinah Shore, Doris Day, Patti Page, Mary Ford, and Georgia Gibbs. Nat King Cole was the only black singer in the top ten— "Too Young" had been on the charts for twenty-two weeks. Sarah Vaughan's version of "These Things I Offer You" was mentioned along with Patti Page's in the list of most popular jukebox plays, though disc jockey reports mention only the white version.

On the sports pages, a Canadian had set a new national pole-vault record of fourteen feet, ten and a half inches, the St. Louis Browns still played at the western edge of the major leagues, and Jackie Robinson was batting .333 for the Brooklyn Dodgers, who still led the National League comfortably, moving like the Titanic toward the fatal playoff with the New York Giants. Joe DiMaggio was in his final season with the New York Yankees. Anyone who wanted to watch Pacific Coast League action in Los Angeles could catch one of five one-stop TWA Constellation flights or one of three on a United DC-6. The state of Oklahoma had its own minor league. Texas had three, the most important three steps down from the majors.

International and national news, if I read it, would have seemed less interesting. The annual polio epidemic made some provincial newspapers but wasn't newsworthy enough for the *New York Times*, and we were so used to avoiding swimming pools and crowds that we took the precautions for granted. Peace talks continued in Korea, as did heavy air strikes, but I was a year away from draft age, and that was an eternity.

President Truman wanted to build our defense strength against the communist threat, but I didn't pay taxes; and though New York had scheduled an air raid drill, even the Boonville chamber of commerce didn't consider our town strategically important. *The Day the Earth Stood Still*, in which an extraterrestrial turns up on the White House lawn to warn both sides about the consequences of their rivalry, seemed as workable a solution to the cold war as any. A lot of other things I didn't pay attention to seem not to have changed in forty years. Israel was having a crisis because of heavy immigration. A *Times* editorial praised "Progress Against Narcotics."

Of course, I didn't see the *Times* that day or any other day for a long time. I'm not sure that I or anyone in my family had heard of it. We had the *Boonville Daily News* and the *Kansas City Times* (morning) and *Kansas City Star* (evening), and dozens of magazines from which to choose, most of which cost fifteen cents.

We also had *Reader's Digest*—a yearly gift from my aunt Cary, which I read almost all the way through every month. The table of contents was predictable. There was a joke about a writer who kept revising his article to try to appeal to the magazine's lasting interests and wound up with "I Had Intercourse with a Teen-Age Bear in an Iron Lung for the FBI and Found God while High on Drugs." The lead article in the September 1951 issue dealt with the dangers of teenage heroin use, another with "Lucky Luciano's New Empire." Three articles on medicine discussed surgical methods, the benefits of group practice, and the life of a circus doctor. At least five articles dealt with cold war issues, though not with Korea, including one on the plight of a Czech priest oppressed by the communists. God had only two articles: "We've Got Faith" and "Take God with You on Monday," which followed "They Shop to Make Your Shopping Pleasanter." On the lighter side was an article on comedian Ed Wynn and one titled "Not So Dumb—the Woodchuck." (Honest to God! You could look it up, as James Thurber said in his story about the

midget baseball player, which, the previous week, had inspired
Bill Veeck to send a real midget to bat for the St. Louis Browns.)

Colliers, a little less predictable or at least more stimulating
than the *Digest*, I usually read at the public library or standing
at the rack at Foster's Drug Store on Main Street. This week
it had a well-illustrated story on "The 1951 Model Blonde" about
an actress with less than fifty minutes of actual screen time
named Marilyn Monroe. It treated her unhappy childhood with
unusual frankness for the period and spoke of her desire to
improve herself intellectually. One writer on the bookshelf by
her bed was Arthur Miller. Joan Crawford, the 1928 model
blonde, was on the back cover endorsing Camel cigarettes as
good for your T-zone, a mysterious region unknown to medical
science which seemed to encompass the throat and lungs.
Another ad, promising "Complete Protection" and illustrated
with a cowboy leering circumspectly at a woman, was sponsored by General Tires. In 1951, only sophisticates or really dirty-
minded teenagers would have suspected a double entendre.

The serial version of Herbert Hoover's memoirs had reached
"Communism Erupts in Europe," but even the Republicans in
my family had never spoken well of the party's last president.
The illustration to an article on Coney Island had an all-white
crowd, just like those at all the public swimming pools in
Missouri. The Los Angeles Rams astonished the sports world
by passing on 53 percent of their offensive plays—453 times in
twelve games.

Of the fiction writers in the issue, only Kurt Vonnegut, Jr.,
is now recognizable. "The Foster Portfolio," narrated by an investment counselor, deals with Horace Foster, a mild-mannered
man with a secret hoard of stocks working multiple jobs in order
to provide luxuries for his family. Raised by a strict mother after
his irresponsible father, a jazz musician, left them, Foster
puzzles the narrator by refusing to touch the money. The counselor tracks Foster to his second job and finds that he is secretly

working under the name of Firehouse Harris as a jazz pianist. If he uses his fortune, he will no longer be able to rationalize his moonlighting. Domesticity as normal; Mom as repressive; jazz as tempting, dangerous freedom; having it both ways: Vonnegut was even then able to use popular themes in a way that seemed radical without being very disturbing.

We may have subscribed to the *Saturday Evening Post*— anyway, like millions of others, I read it most weeks. To offset *Reader's Digest*, the *Post* ran articles on silicosis and "The Arrogant Doctor" and, in contrast to the *Digest's* shoppers, "Four Thousand Women Ringing Doorbells" as welcome wagon hostesses to greet the increasing number of relocated homeowners. While it was reported that in Tulsa, Oklahoma, "The Relief Chiselers Are Stealing Us Blind," a customs agent boasted that "Smugglers Were My Quarry," especially celebrities bringing in luxury goods. Like *Colliers*, this week's issue of the *Post* had a Western short story. A Packard Patrician, top of the line, was advertised at $3586.

Life, which boasted a circulation over 5,200,000, was pretty dull that week except for Gina Lollobrigida on the cover and some other Italian actresses inside. An article praised singer Herb Jeffries for refusing to pass as white and was illustrated by photographs of black-white celebrity marriages. I had heard Jeffries on the radio and didn't care about his color, but I could see that being white, or thought to be white, had considerable advantages; and it was unusually liberal of the magazine to run an objective story on what some people still called miscegenation. There was mention of a defense contract to build an atomic submarine.

Look, the imitation of *Life*, didn't give its circulation figures, but, like the *Digest*, promised "Better Health for Millions" through prepaid medical care, worried about the readiness of Eisenhower's forces in Europe, and had an article on the well-known comedian Jack E. Leonard, a veteran of burlesque houses.

Its atomic story noted, "We're Spending Billions on the Atom" and asked, "What Are We Buying?" The answer was reassuring. *Life* had featured newly rich farmers in the San Joaquin Valley; *Look* was interested in "California Money-Makers" who sold U-Bild Patterns. Sugar Ray Robinson promised "I'll Be Back" after losing his middleweight boxing title to Randy Turpin, a white Englishman. Another article wondered "When Should Teenagers Fall in Love?" and provided a twenty-five question quiz and quite sensible advice to help them decide.

The quiz was flanked by a Formfit Bra ad, with a model—drawn, not photographed—peering coyly over a coffee cup and wearing an industrial strength model that promised fit not only according to bust and cup size but *"degree of separation*—wide, medium or narrow" to provide greater glamor, comfort, and freedom.

I wanted all of those qualities, though I was more interested in the contents than the engineering of the package—if I allowed myself to think about them, which, as a good Catholic boy, I wasn't supposed to. I had never touched a bra, let alone a breast. My knowledge of sex was entirely theoretical, and sketchy at that.

That didn't outrun my knowledge of most other things. Neither I nor anybody I knew had flown on a commercial airliner. Except for Sir Laurence Olivier's *Hamlet*, I had never seen a foreign film. I wouldn't have recognized marijuana if I saw it; I hardly knew any Democrats, except my father, let alone a communist; I had met one Jew, whose defensiveness about his religion or race or whatever it was merely puzzled me. I knew that some people thought that Catholics were a separate breed, partly because I had been told that from the pulpit and in Catholic schools since I could remember.

But like a number of my contemporaries in Boonville and across the country, I was tired of the small-town "we," and I thought I was ready for a larger stage and a lead role in first-

11

person singular. The official record at Boonville Catholic High School, from which I had graduated in May, seemed to justify my confidence. I played lead roles in the junior and senior plays; lettered in two sports; served on yearbook and newspaper staffs; won a medal for having the highest grades in religion; had been valedictorian. Of course, the dramatic roles had been the result not of histrionic talent but of my ability to memorize; the athletic teams had losing records; all seventeen members of my graduating class had some part in putting together the yearbook; the religion medal was, to an adolescent boy, more an embarrassment than an honor; as valedictorian of a class that size, I was not only in the top ten percent, I was the only whole person in the top ten percent.

It was gratifying to be valedictorian because townspeople who paid any attention at all were surprised that I finished ahead of a boy who not only came from a family notorious for its academic achievements but was the best athlete in our class. I was glad to be able to beat him at something. My mother was pleased because her competitive instincts had been aroused, and in 1951, women didn't have many outlets for those, except bridge, where she excelled, and housekeeping, where she was a nonstarter. My father was pleased because his older brother was supposed—especially by himself—to be smarter, and reports from their hometown indicated surprise that this branch of the Davises had demonstrated academic competence of any kind. When my father heard the news—even if he suspected that Grandpa Murray had made it up, as he was quite capable of doing—he grinned in pleasure. He rarely smiled at anything; as far as I knew, he had never before smiled at anything I had done. That was a lot better than the religion medal.

The medal didn't mean that I was particularly devout, though I did believe in hell and, less firmly, in heaven. And my selection as valedictorian didn't mean that I was well educated. In fact, my transcript was thoroughly fraudulent. The 93.75 average in four math courses may reflect some effort, but except for geometry, where I could see what was happening on the paper in front of me, I had no idea what was going on or why. I averaged only a point higher in English, and that meant I could spell almost everything correctly, remember the grammar that had been drilled into us for years, skim through the assignments, and spend the rest of my time reading something interesting and highly unofficial.

As far as I could tell, anything described as education consisted of embalmed facts, conventional pieties, and flowery language to cover stale emotions. Because I had finished eighth in a statewide competitive examination for a scholarship to the University of Missouri (including subjects like economics of which even our principal had barely heard), no one realized that I had developed the worst study habits of any valedictorian in the state and probably the world because the education I was offered seemed to have no bearing on anything I wanted to do or be.

What I wanted to be was a newspaperman, partly because I thought I had more talent for writing than for anything else, partly because Bill Corum, a sportswriter, was the only person from Boonville to become anything like a national figure, and partly because E. J. Melton, owner and editor of the weekly *Cooper County Record*, was the closest thing to a model I could imagine—he made his living by annoying people with his writing. Working on the *Record* as apprentice printer, reporter, mailer, and floor sweeper had not dimmed the glamor that I attached to the profession. Of course, I had no idea how to get from where I was to the role of star reporter. And what I wanted to do was to leave Boonville for a world where people saw and did new and interesting things.

Postponing History

Wanting out is a common ambition in small towns all over America. In 1951, there were three ways to realize it. One was to get a job in the big city—in my case, either Kansas City or St. Louis, at the edges of the imaginable world. At sixteen, I was too young for this, and besides, I had no idea of what I could do.

A second way—chosen by four men from the class ahead of me—was to enlist in a branch of military service or volunteer for the draft. That would get you even farther from home and pile up educational benefits under the GI Bill. But there was a war—or police action, as it was called—in progress in Korea.

I was not a pacifist, but there didn't seem to be much point in joining up even if I had been old enough, which I wasn't. If I had looked a year ahead, I could have taken comfort in a *Saturday Evening Post* article of September 8, 1951: "What Happens When You're Drafted Now?" Except for the haircuts and unavoidable inconveniences, it said, the new army wasn't a bit like the old army.

Fortunately, a third alternative to work and military service was just beginning to open up to people—mostly men—of my class and region: college.

For the older generation, a college education might be a badge of status (we were never explicitly told this), but except for men in the professional classes and women teachers, it didn't seem necessary in order to make a decent living and have a solid place in the community. One obviously successful father of a friend might have been to college, though my brother doubts it. None of my college-bound classmates' parents had. One father ran a filling station, one owned a barber shop, one was a game warden, and mine traded cars and cattle. Attendance at college was rare for graduates of Boonville Catholic High School. Once the nuns brought to assembly a man who was going to night school in Kansas City to show us that it was possible.

Looking back, it is obvious that family tradition mattered less than wider social currents. All of a sudden it was time for couples who had married just in time for the Depression and survived World War II on the home front to send their sons, and less often daughters, to college. The class ahead of mine—born in 1932, before the birthrate nose-dived—had thirty-one students, but only one of the eleven males went straight to college, and perhaps two of the females. In my class, four of eight males did, and three of those went on to do graduate work. None of the females went to college, though several went into nursing programs. But having gone up, the numbers stayed up.

Although at the time even our parents probably did not try to generalize, there are a number of ways to explain this sudden change during the late 1940s. A million men, many from classes that would have considered high school the end of the line, had taken advantage of the GI Bill to get a college education and other kinds of training. The postwar boom in housing and all kinds of hard goods made people who had come through the Depression feel even more prosperous than they were. They wanted their children to have a better life, and college was the most obvious way to see that they got it.

We didn't think in those terms, of course, and our parents didn't talk in them, at least to us. The closest I heard to a general reflection was my father's refrain, at first confident and then a little more plaintive each year I spent in graduate school, "Education is something they can never take away from you." Sending your son to college or your daughter to nursing school—the pattern we were familiar with—was an investment in the future.

I can't remember when I assumed that I would go to college, but probably there was no one moment in which my parents announced it or I received a flash of private revelation. College was not unknown in my extended family. Neither of my parents had gone past high school, but my father's much older half-sister had a degree in music education and had done at least some graduate work; my two older cousins had degrees in architecture and engineering; and well back down the family tree there were, though I didn't learn this until much later, preachers and even a theologian who was master of a Cambridge college at the end of the sixteenth century. Grandpa Murray, my mother's father, attended a commercial school after getting his diploma, and he obviously valued learning or—the same thing in Cooper County, Missouri, at that time—he read a lot of books.

The question of where to go to college didn't seem to come up. For one thing, there was less choice than there is now. Many state universities had been located in out-of-the-way towns like Columbia, Missouri; Boulder, Colorado; Bloomington, Indiana; Berkeley, California, which they dominated and which served as depositories or reservations for the moderately affluent, mostly male, student population, under the unspoken assumption that a fringe benefit of educating a late adolescent was getting him off your hands for four years.

What had begun as normal schools, or teacher-training institutions, might be named after a town (Emporia State in Kansas) or a secondary point on the compass (Northeast Missouri State, various Southwestern States) to indicate geographical distribution and a regional clientele. But residents of St. Louis—and of many of the cities that then boasted major league baseball teams—would have found it difficult to get a bachelor's degree from a publicly supported institution in their home town.

For one thing, the upscale market had been preempted by places like Washington University of St. Louis, Harvard, the Universities of Chicago, Cincinnati, and Pennsylvania, which in origin were WASP and to some extent remain so in spirit. Except for a few places like the City College of New York and Brooklyn College, there was little government interest in the downscale market.

All of these schools were unimaginably remote, geographically and intellectually, but I never considered a regional state school because I certainly didn't want to be a teacher. The University of Missouri (known as MU), only twenty miles away, seemed the obvious choice, though it was large, secular, and otherwise intimidating.

I knew even less about the what than I did the where. No one I knew well enough to talk to seriously could tell me what it was like. The nuns at the high school indicated that college courses were much more difficult than those in high school and that we would have to work much harder and more independently. Since nothing else they told us was even remotely interesting, we paid very little attention.

Monsignor Roels, the pastor of our parish, who was often worth listening to, had told the senior boys during a particularly solemn talk that he doubted there was a single virgin at the University of Missouri. I was prepared to believe him because two brothers (who attended Central College and worked part-time at the local Buick dealership where my father managed sales and my mother kept books) had taken me to a NAIA basketball final in Kansas City and then to a party with college girls in a hotel room. I was awed by the style and scent of these women and by the offhand way in which the men referred to the probable disposition of their legs during sexual intercourse. This level of daring, sophistication, and freedom from religious constraints was heady but daunting, and I was secretly relieved when, over my nominal protests, the brothers decided that it would be better to take me back to Boonville than to try to explain the alternative to my mother. If this was college life, I wasn't sure that I was ready for it.

I had other, less tangential experience with colleges. I had lived a block away from Kemper Military Academy, which had a junior college. No one from Boonville would have thought of going there, even if we could have afforded it, but it was a real campus with a lot of brick and pillars and even some ivy. Fifteen miles away in Fayette, Central College (now Central Methodist) looked even more like a movie set because the buildings were lower and separated by expanses of lawn, and we saw it only during summers when those intimidating women had left.

But to most people in Boonville, MU was the archetype of what a college should be. My father had taken my scout troop to usher at MU football games, and the size of the stadium and the sophistication of the crowd made the experience qualitatively different from the public high school and Kemper games I had watched. This was the big time, or at least the Big Six, and when we stopped at the sorority house of a friend's older sister, the casual glamor of these strange beings was so overwhelming that I could not even think of them as objects of desire.

MU was so unimaginably large—it had almost ten thousand students, over 80 percent of them male, while Boonville had a total population of six thousand—that it even had two campuses, red and white. The older red one was disposed around a huge quadrangle, with large white pillars standing picturesquely at one end. It looked like an expensive Hollywood set.

At the other end stood the Walter Williams School of Journalism, the first in the country and the finest in the region. It had its own daily newspaper, put out by the students, thicker than the Boonville *Daily News* I had once delivered. It even had its own printing plant.

The summer after my junior year I had attended a week-long workshop for high school journalists. I don't remember a thing they tried to teach me, but I was impressed by the spacious building, quiet in the summer, with the arch between its two wings.

During my senior year I assumed that I would go to MU and major in journalism, and the summer after I graduated I went to a Sigma Nu rush party on the invitation of an unimaginably daring graduate of Boonville High who reportedly spent weekends with women at Lake Taneycomo. The members seemed incredibly sophisticated, but the other prospective pledges—most of them named Bob, too—didn't seem too intimidating. The previous summer I had gone to Boys' State, sponsored by the American Legion to instill principles of democratic government and back-room maneuvering and I had learned that even people from St. Louis were not totally alien. I think I was the only one who got drunk enough to throw up. That was better preparation for college than I realized.

I hadn't enrolled or, I think, even applied to MU, but that was no problem because, like every other college in 1951, it was not in a position to be choosy. Most of the veterans from World War II who attended on the GI Bill had left schools that had expanded to accommodate them. The bill itself expired in July 1951; and the normal freshman class had been born in 1933, when the birthrate was the lowest it had ever been.

About this time my mother learned that Rockhurst College in Kansas City would give a partial scholarship for tuition to valedictorians from Catholic high schools. I don't know what else she found out, but Rockhurst was reassuringly Catholic, or at least, as the inside joke went, Jesuit. While she didn't know much about religious orders, Jesuits had a high recognition factor because they were a large organization of which Rockhurst was a very small part.

But it was typical of Jesuit higher education because, unlike state universities cloistered away in small towns, most Jesuit and other Catholic colleges were located in large cities. In the nineteenth and early twentieth centuries, when most of them were founded, that's where the successive waves of Catholic immigrants located.

When I was ready to matriculate, these schools were still conscious of their original mission. Two years before I entered Rockhurst, the English novelist Evelyn Waugh, hardly a populist, toured America for *Life* to get an outsider's view of the American Catholic church. He was pleasantly astonished at the American system of Catholic education for "boldly asserting that nothing less than an entire Christian education is necessary to produce Christians." And though he was often branded as a snob, he saw nothing wrong with the desire "to transform a proletariat into a bourgeoisie; to produce a faithful laity, qualified to take its part in the general life of the nation."

Like many of Waugh's statements, this was precise, succinct, and far more candid than its subjects might wish. However, he did not explore the contradictions between spiritual and secular life, and most Catholic educators were not anxious to do so. Catholics, and not just the hierarchy, were nervous about the effect of secularism on good Catholic upbringing, but some of them were eager to prove that Catholics could be as good, and as normal, as anyone else and to escape what was beginning to be called the "ghetto mentality," although Catholics had built and maintained their own walls. This attitude lies behind the Rockhurst dean's recruiting letter of March 1954, addressed "Dear Young American," which challenges the recipient to opt for "a college education that is a challenge instead of a pleasure cruise" in order "to be one of the leaders in building a greater America and a better world" and join other "red-blooded Americans," many of whom "are just average Joes scholastically." The letter mentions God-given abilities and four hundred years of Jesuit education, but Catholicism is nowhere mentioned.

However, Catholic higher education was ghettoized culturally. All Catholics had to consider the Legion of Decency's ranking of movies, some of the most interesting being rated "Morally Objectionable in Part for All." All Catholics were forbidden to read any work or author on the Index of Prohibited Books, which included *Madame Bovary* and everything by Voltaire, Sartre, and other philosophers most Catholics were unlikely to encounter. Books by Catholic authors were recommended, and sometimes students were herded into courses on Great Catholic Writers.

In fact, like their secular contemporaries, Catholic college students could ignore the world outside, including the ordinary life of the church, for weeks at a time because college was itself a kind of ghetto, or, to put it in Christian terms, a cloister. And one way to keep people inside walls is to make them feel superior to those outside the walls. Catholic schools tried to foster this attitude. The Jesuits tried hardest.

The Society of Jesus, the official name of the Jesuits, was the most ostentatiously successful and elitist religious order involved in American education. The Jesuit motto is *Ad Majorem Dei Gloriam*, to the greater glory of God, and like Stephen Dedalus in James Joyce's *A Portrait of the Artist as a Young Man*, students in the order's schools headed all class papers with the Latin initials *AMDG*. The order's unofficial motto was, supposedly, "Give me the boy, and I will be responsible for the man." "Responsible" is a nice, equivocal word that, as the occasional Jesuit skeptic would point out, covered the order's effect on Voltaire, who operated under an assumed name, and Joyce, who was too proud to and displayed an odd sense of brand snobbery in favor of the order of priests who taught him. Both men were international in range; they needed to be because they had a tendency to make any given place too hot for them.

So had the Jesuits. Founded in the sixteenth century by a military man, they were organized on military lines—the head of the order still has the title of general—and emphasized not learning for its own sake but as a weapon in the service of God. They were elite troops who took a special vow of fealty to the Pope, and each member underwent long and rigorous training before he was ordained a priest. They were thought to consider themselves better than other religious orders of priests, and at least one Jesuit spoke to me dismissively of the so-called secular priests—the ones who did not belong to orders and did most of the parish work in the United States—as little more than administrators. To see the other side, one had only to watch a Jesuit attempt to preside at a wedding or other ceremony commonplace for a parish priest. Chaos reigned because, as Evelyn Waugh discovered in rehearsals for his wedding two decades earlier on the other side of the Atlantic, Jesuits were "sensationally ignorant of simplest professional duties."

In the early 1950s, the Jesuits were quite comfortably placed, and less successful rivals attributed this to their discovery that rich people have souls, too. Any large city with a considerable Catholic population would have a number of Catholic high schools (sports page headlines reading "St. Ambrose Stomps Mater Dei" would not even draw a chuckle), but the Jesuit high school—which admitted only boys—would almost certainly have the highest academic and social standing. Students and alumni of St. Louis University High, for example, referred to their school as "*the* High." One of my colleagues still does so, forty years after his graduation. The Jesuit schools were the closest the American Catholic educational system came to prep schools; and by the early 1950s, their best graduates could gain entrance to any college their parents could afford.

Some went to Jesuit colleges, but with a few exceptions these did not have the same status as the high schools. For one thing, the colleges faced stiffer local and regional competition. For another, most of them had a different mission and clientele. But for Americans, Catholic or not, education has been a symbol of upward mobility, and no one was better able to manipulate these symbols than the Jesuits. They had always been expert merchandisers, and they founded colleges in the big Catholic markets: Washington, D.C., New York, Baltimore, Chicago, New Orleans, Kansas City, Buffalo, Denver, Omaha, Los Angeles, and other places where the order could use its forces most effectively. Most of the schools were named after Jesuit saints (Loyola, Marquette, Gonzaga) or the cities in which they were located (St. Louis, San Francisco, Boston). The name

Rockhurst came from the happy blend of Stoneyhurst, the English Jesuit boarding school, and, according to the most recent Rockhurst catalog, "the rocky hill which provided both its foundation and the stone for its early buildings." There was probably some recognition of the commercially named Rockhill area, which is hard to dissociate from William Rockhill Nelson of the Kansas City *Star*.

Rockhurst wasn't the oldest or the largest or the best Jesuit school, but the administration frequently reminded us that the college was part of the Jesuit system. They didn't have to because in Conway Hall, the chief classroom building, there was a large map indicating the location of all twenty-seven Jesuit colleges and universities. One of my contemporaries remarked that it looked like something you'd find in the offices of a chain store.

As in any good chain, local market considerations were carefully studied. Part of an undated recruiting brochure— probably late 1940s, judging from the hairstyles and the pre-ponderance of neckties in the photos—asks and answers questions along the lines of the catechism all Catholics were taught. The questions:

1. Can you plan your future in these unsettled times?
2. Why go out of town to college?
3. Do local colleges offer good opportunities?
4. Does Rockhurst offer you the extra-curricular activities that you want?
5. What advantages does Rockhurst offer you in its educational standing?
6. Does training *by men* and *with men* mean more to you?
7. Is Rockhurst modern in outlook? Attentive to your particular needs?

> 8. Does Rockhurst seek to build men by forming character?
> 9. Can Rockhurst College mean all this to you?
> 10. What will it cost you to attend Rockhurst College?

The questions and answers cover four pages, and anyone trained to examine a sales pitch will hear a persistent defensive undertone. There is a clear sense that some potential customers hesitate to send their sons to college at all. If they do, many out-of-town schools (probably the Universities of Kansas and Missouri) are larger, more prestigious, or both; are not segregated by sex; and offer more obvious preparation for the modern world.

Some of the answers play directly on greed and fear, two very practical considerations, particularly for parents who are making sacrifices to send their sons to college. The answer to question two—why go out of town?—suggests, rather diffidently, that the student might become interested in professional school, but it argues that he should stay in Kansas City because he will live and work there the rest of his life and should begin making "invaluable contacts" as soon as possible. Another is that his parents can keep an eye on him—or, in brochurese, provide "the salutary and refining influence of his parents and of his home."

The answers to questions eight and nine are supposed to be the clinchers. Eight is obviously aimed not at students but at the people who were going to pay the bills and who might—especially in view of the postwar Red scare and growing distrust of intellectuals—feel uneasy about providing unforeseen opportunities to their sons:

> 8. Does Rockhurst seek to build men by forming character?

25

The nation is becoming aware of the unfortunate results of a century of education which has deliberately omitted God from its program. Parents are becoming increasingly aware of the necessity that schools do more than merely impart knowledge. Colleges can build men only by building character.

The only schools in America which have accepted this responsibility as a fixed part of their program are the church-affiliated schools and colleges. Parents whose sons have graduated from Rockhurst appreciate this fact!

Character building is fostered at Rockhurst through classes in philosophy and religion, through the relations of student and teacher, student and counselor, through student activities—methods which constitute the tradition of Rockhurst.

Question nine—Can Rockhurst College mean all this to you?—is answered hind-side-to: "One does not have to attend a large university to get a good college education. Rockhurst College, although a comparatively small school [four hundred to five hundred day students when I was there], nevertheless possesses all the essential qualities of a good college." The material about four hundred years of Jesuit education and the chain of Jesuit colleges and universities is buried in the next two paragraphs—hardly an emphatic position.

I don't know if Mom read any of this material—I didn't until four decades later—and neither of us had seen the place, but she probably made some shrewd guesses. Since I was not yet seventeen, she decided that somebody ought to be responsible for her boy and that I needed more, and more responsible, supervision than I would get in a dormitory or fraternity house. She may also have thought that my transition from a high school with seventy-five students would be easier if I went to a college with 460 students rather than to a university twenty times that size. It seems probable that she expected my Catholic faith to be better preserved at Rockhurst than at the notoriously secular university, and perhaps—her faith was strong though selective—she was influenced by the rule of the church that every student must attend a Catholic school when that was possible.

Although I was informed of her decision, I wasn't consulted. Probably I could have gone to the University of Missouri if I had really insisted, but I may have had doubts about being able to handle all that sophistication. Besides, out of Boonville was out of Boonville, as far as I was concerned, and one of the two poles of urbanity to which small-town Missouri youth gravitated was Kansas City. My father, a renegade Presbyterian, didn't seem to care one way or another. He had promised when he married Mom that any children would be raised Catholics, and in any case, he was most unlikely to object to stronger measures of discipline. Besides, Mom's salaried job was intended to pay for the children's education, and if she had to pay, she had the say. And anyway, unlike my mother's side of the family, if he had no information on a subject, he didn't venture an opinion about it.

Having made her decision, Mom launched into an orgy of shopping that produced, as college equipment and birthday presents, various objects of which, forty years later, I remember only a portable typewriter, a largely superfluous electric razor, a portable AM radio with numerous vacuum tubes the size of a small boom-box, a bomber jacket (suede turned out to be more fashionable, but mine was more practical because, I discovered, it was easier to clean of vomit), a reinforced cardboard box with crossing straps and a place to insert an address card in which I was to mail home my laundry, and a leather suitcase. (I still have the suitcase, but it is too large to carry on an airplane and too small to be worth checking through.)

We loaded up the car and made the two-and-a-half-hour drive, familiar as far as Linwood Boulevard, where U.S. Highway 40 entered Kansas City and up to the Paseo, where we sometimes turned south to go to the Swope Park zoo and outdoor theater. That was a little out of our way, but it was worth the detour because Paseo was unlike any street we had ever seen—two separate streets divided by a green, landscaped strip.

A few blocks west was Troost Avenue, which didn't have a divider strip or any other sign of green. The Paseo was for show; Troost was a working street. It had streetcar tracks, and it was lined with a bewildering variety of small businesses and clothing stores and bars and restaurants for twenty-five blocks until it crossed a concrete-lined creek and headed uphill. I had looked forward to being in the city, but this looked like an infinite extension of Boonville's Main Street, no less boring and far more alien.

Rockhurst College was a bit more reassuring. Across the street stood a church shaped like a stylized fish (from the Greek pun for Christ's initials) rather than in the traditional cross pattern. What I could see of the college itself, two stone buildings, looked rather like MU's white campus, but the campus didn't look anything like a movie set, and I didn't even think about what role I might play there.

I had been instructed to report to Brebeuf Lodge, located on the southeast corner of the campus on Fifty-third Street between Daniel and Chabanel Lodges. These names—of Jesuit martyrs in North America, we later learned, and speculated the following winter that they had frozen to death—sounded exotic, even to someone accustomed to place-names like Chouteau Springs and Petit Saline creek that dotted the Cooper County map.

The three lodges did look like they belonged on a set—for *Stalag 17* or something even grimmer. Behind a six-foot chain-link fence topped with three strands of barbed wire, in the far southwest corner of the campus, below the football field and south of a bare expanse that turned out to be the baseball and intramural fields, squatted three one-story buildings covered with grayish tar paper, each with four rudimentary porches. Obviously they were government issue, and they didn't look a thing like the Sigma Nu house or anything I had seen at Kemper or Central College. They were known as the barracks.

I don't remember whether my mother was allowed to go inside, but if she was, she was the only woman I ever saw there. But then mothers were not exactly women, though not exactly not. I think she did meet the Reverend Joseph A. McCallin, S.J., the prefect in charge of the three lodges. She was probably reassured by the fact that he looked rather like an ascetic Bing Crosby and had a high-pitched voice a lot like my militant atheist grandfather Murray's.

Then she left me with my newly acquired gear, my unfortunate study habits, and almost complete ignorance, on the edge of the big world I wanted to enter—or anyway Kansas City, a hundred miles from home and seventy-five times more populous, where, as the song in *Oklahoma* promised, they'd gone about as far as they could go.

Raw Material

A valuable part of a young man's education is the salutary and refining influence of his parents and of his home.
—Rockhurst College brochure

"Oh, I shouldn't try to teach them anything, not just yet, anyway. Just keep them quiet."
—Evelyn Waugh, Decline and Fall

Where neither words nor the corrector avail and some student is seen to be incorrigible and a scandal to others, it is better to dismiss him from the schools rather than to keep him where he himself is not progressing and others are receiving harm. This decision will be left to the rector of the university, that everything may proceed in a manner conducive to the glory and service to God our Lord.
—The Constitutions of the Society of Jesus

Colleges now spend a great deal more time and money recruiting students than they did in 1951, and the orientation given to the ones who show up devotes more time to social

30

and study habits than was the case forty years ago. But otherwise things have not changed markedly: the students arrange themselves into groups according to taste, inclination, point of origin, and place of residence. And in the initial stages, academic interests and intellectual capacity have little influence on who joins which group.

I probably remember as much of my formal orientation as the freshmen who had it last fall, which is to say almost nothing. We were given placement tests—I wound up in the "high" sections of several required courses, separated from my new colleagues in the barracks. A variety of people droned on about various topics—"liberal education" was a recurrent motif—but the theater where we assembled was hot, we were more curious about our new peers than about the official subjects of discussion, and nobody said anything about what we really wanted to know: where to find girls and parties.

Later, the sophomore class, or its more testosterone-filled members, conducted initiation. This involved giving the bookstore whatever it charged for the blue-and-white beanies we were required to wear and taking off letter sweaters and other mementos of our high schools. Then we had to give nominal obedience to some rules I have now forgotten and take a few swats with paddles if we broke them, both administered by the members of the sophomore class who enjoyed that sort of thing. The purpose, aside from making the sophomores feel important, was apparently to remind us that we were now college men and should put away childish things—though in the first case we had already been told that six times a day during orientation and, in the second, wearing a beanie seemed counterproductive.

Today someone would probably seek an injunction, but then we just bought the beanies and later, led by some of the stronger personalities in our class, staged a minor rebellion not long after classes started. After a kangaroo court was held, everybody forgot the whole thing. The initiation process had given the freshmen some sense of unity: everyone, no matter where we came from, thought beanies incredibly stupid. (The following year, no one I knew took part in conducting initiation, and I didn't know it had in fact occurred until years later.)

But in a way, this process was effective. I put away my Boonville Catholic High School letter sweater, probably because it identified my point of origin. And the freshman class did come together in minor rebellion against the sophomores, after which the mild persecution ceased.

However, the process did not immediately abolish old lines of division. In those days, Rockhurst College did almost no recruiting outside the range of the greater Kansas City public transportation system, and most of the freshmen arrived in clusters from the Catholic high schools. For the first year or so, people were identified by where they had gone to school. The Rockhurst High contingent, if not the largest, was the best organized and most influential because they were already familiar with the Jesuit system and, since the college and high school shared the campus and the cafeteria, the literal territory. And Rockhurst High attracted students from all over the city because of its strong academic and athletic programs. The other Catholic high schools were regional. A large group came from Hogan High School, ten blocks away on Sixty-third Street, as far south as Catholic secondary education reached; Lillis, De La Salle, and Glennon provided diminishing cadres proportionate to their distance from the college. Regardless of high school affiliation, the locals distinguished between Yankees and Confederates, depending on whether they lived north or south of Thirty-ninth Street. A number of the Rockhurst High group were Yankees.

But to the boarding students, the natives looked pretty much alike. And we to them. For one thing, we came from strange and outlandish places like Puerto Rico, Maryville, Kansas, and Boonville, Missouri. Our living arrangements were odd and chaotic. The man who became my best friend at Rockhurst—a Lillis graduate—recently commented that his only memories of visits to the barracks were of constant noise, smoke, and card games. But then he had the salutary and refining influence of his parents and home. We had the sense that the locals regarded us as inferior.

Since we had to be different, we tried to make the difference into a badge of distinction. White people hadn't yet learned the word "funk," but the barracks had all the marks. The interior decor was war surplus. There were communal showers and toilets in the middle; four hallways with gas stoves (the only heat), couches, and alcoves for closets on each side; two rooms off each hallway. We had army surplus bunks, painted brown; desks, painted gray; nondescript chairs. The walls were painted pale, army surplus green.

Across campus stood Hanley House, the only other living quarters for out-of-town students. It had in fact been a house, while the barracks had never been lodges in anything but imagination. But we came to feel that they had an antistyle that none of us would have traded for real walls and central heat. Our prefect had a Ph.D. in history; theirs was the athletic director. The barracks not only had character, they had characters.

We thought of ourselves as barracks boys. The term "male bonding" had not been coined, but the behavior it describes— males doing really stupid things in a group—was well established. With the help of some bad models, we tended to reinforce each other's less fortunate tendencies. Or perhaps I was more impressionable and tried harder to fit in.

The platoon movie was already a cliché. After forty years and *An Officer and a Gentleman* and *Stripes* and a host of other uses, the format is still popular because it reflects the experience of being set down in a new environment—summer camp, college, basic training, even a cruise—with a lot of other people with whom one has in common only the necessity of adapting to a preexisting and powerful organization.

We new barracks boys thought of ourselves as very different from each other, but most of us were from Kansas or Missouri and had gone to Catholic high schools and—except for the St. Louis U-High graduates, who regarded themselves as superior to everyone in the barracks, the college, and probably the universe—had gone to coed schools taught by nuns. Among the people in the group I joined there were two Johns, a Bill, and a Jim. Only one of us had, or admitted to having, a girlfriend back home. Many of us (I am guessing, because we never talked about this kind of thing) were the first in our families to go to college. Our parents were solidly established but not affluent. I'm not sure whether the college allowed freshmen to have cars, but none of my group did, nor did most of the upperclassmen.

We did have some real exotics: a Puerto Rican so upper-class that his sister was blonde; a Kentuckian with a Roman numeral after his name who lived as though the *code duello* still operated and looked like a lean, mean Ashley Wilkes; one local, convicted as an accessory to armed robbery, who lived in the barracks as a condition of his parole, studied opera, and looked a little like Edward G. Robinson.

Like the locals, we sorted ourselves into subgroups. The people with the most urban accents were at the top of the social scale; those with the most rural, at the bottom. One boy had an even more incomprehensible accent than mine and was mocked for saying, "You-all boys got any say-zors?" I wasn't about to claim solidarity with another hick, I'm ashamed to say, and he was gone by the end of orientation week.

By then I had become part of an identifiable group that included the tallest and shortest of the St. Louis contingent;

my roommate, a high school quarterback from south central Missouri; and sometimes the Kentuckian and the mid-sized U-High graduate; and occasionally the Puerto Rican and Florian Muckenthaler, a name I feel free to use because I have no discreditable stories to tell about him.

It's hard to see what brought us together for that first year. Some of the room assignments made sense: two U-High people; two high school lettermen from small towns. But the only obvious thing the four of us had in common was that we wanted at the same time to act like college students and to hold on to the tastes and attitudes we brought with us because, in so much change, they were familiar.

The administration made some attempt to act *in loco parentis*. Most people who went to college before 1960, however ignorant of Latin, know what that means: the school stands in the place of a parent, and an old-fashioned parent at that, the kind that set curfews and sent you to your room when you misbehaved. The system disappeared in the 1960s, about the time that real parents of that kind went the way of dinosaurs, partly because of student protests but mostly because administrators were delighted to be rid of a thankless and hopeless job.

The major object of the old rules was to return the clients to their parents more or less in the same moral condition in which they arrived: girls without illegitimate babies and boys without criminal records. In other words, preventive detention for moral purposes. (Now the emphasis is on counseling and rehabilitation: some universities offer workshops for students who have trouble with study habits, meeting deadlines, and a host of other academic behavioral problems.)

As the quotation about "salutary and refining influence" implied, the Rockhurst administration preferred to leave that to people crazy enough to be real parents. But the Jesuits had very clear ideas about fallen human nature, and in 1951 the rules we were given made an attempt to curb it.

My children would think them medieval. The Jesuits dated from the Renaissance, not the Middle Ages, but the rules for freshmen living on campus, made clear to us the first week, would cause riots even in a minimum security prison. We had to be in our rooms from 7:00 to 9:00 P.M. and after 10:00 P.M. every night before class days. We could stay out until midnight (or was it 1:00 A.M.?) on Friday nights and until 11:00 P.M. on Saturday nights, since of course we were supposed to get up for Sunday mass. And I thought my father was strict!

The rules were enforced by another kind of father—Father McCallin—assisted by an older student called a proctor. If we broke the rules, we might be "campused"—that is, forbidden to leave the barracks even during those free times—or given lesser penalties like written exercises of a certain length or poems to memorize. (Assigned Rudyard Kipling's "Danny Deever," I made the mistake of showing up fifteen minutes later to recite it. The next time I was assigned Francis Thompson's "The Hound of Heaven," which is a hell of a lot longer and has a more confusing meter and rhyme scheme. This was further proof that it does not pay to be a smart-ass.) You could come in as drunk as you liked, but possession of alcohol on the premises was punishable—and in one instance was punished—by immediate expulsion. The authorities never conducted a search, which was fortunate for the enrollment figures, and it was assumed that students knew how to be circumspect.

It is tempting to exaggerate the repressiveness of the system. The prefect told us the rules, expected us to remember them, and enforced them as judge and jury not subject to appeal, and then, except for some tactfully oblique advice and occasional removal of suggestive materials from the walls of our rooms, pretty much left us alone. He and the proctor told us when to quiet down and turn out lights but not when to get up or what to wear or what to do during study periods. The real business of turning us into prominent Catholic laymen or at least petit bourgeoisie well-grounded in faith and morals was supposed to take place up the hill and in the classroom.

The flaw in this assumption—and more liberal policies have not corrected it—is that, in the absence of the salutary and refining influence of home and family, and in spite or because of rules, young people form substitute and often dysfunctional families.

The values of our new family were not those promoted during orientation week or the barracks rules but those of our immediate predecessors, like unruly older brothers. To the immature eye, the most interesting upperclassmen were the most flamboyant, and my vision was far from 20/20 physically or socially. On our first day, several of us were listening to a sophomore give us his accumulated wisdom, probably about how to evade barracks rules, when we heard a horn outside. A girl with a car had come to pick him up, and he sauntered out as if this were entirely natural. Anyone who could reverse roles like that must have incredible social (translate, as, overtly, we did not, sexual) power.

One of his friends actually had a car—a 1930s-vintage green Ford with the top cut off in which he would roar off and squeal back. Sometimes it wouldn't run and often it was short of gas, but it was a car, and it looked like nothing we had seen. We listened with awe to the tale of a double date in which his closest friend had vomited on his date—"It wasn't as though he couldn't find a window!" Why were we impressed? Latent hostility toward women or the idea of women that had been impressed on us? Awe at the sheer anarchic outrageousness? A lot of both was going around in the early 1950s; this expression of it gave us a glimpse of what, in our innocence, we thought was an entirely different world.

In fact, the pattern of the Whole Man given us by the barracks sophomores was like a bad country-Western song, a modified machismo that involved steady drinking, some womanizing within the limits of time and place, and swearing—not all that different from what older boys in Boonville, especially those from the public high school, had reportedly done to inspire my awe and envy. But now college men were doing these things, so that must be what college men did. Of course, there were some qualifications. Seriously committed drunks and lovers were mutually exclusive categories, and successful ladies' men did not swear in front of women.

It was not easy to meet barracks standards. As freshmen, we couldn't always drink because we might be short of money or, if it was near election time, the liquor inspectors were checking IDs. We might not have girlfriends for any number of reasons. But we could certainly swear, and critical standards were exacting. One upperclassman burst from his room in frustration and repeated "fuck" about fifteen times. A French student leaned out of his room to observe, shrugged, and said, "These Americans! They don't know how to swear." Later the Puerto Rican classmate, who had come to Rockhurst to perfect his English, came out with the carefully rehearsed "I'll be a dirty motherfucking, cocksucking son of a bitch. There! I said it!" The vocabulary was only a basis. Energy was important. Style was necessary. Understatement, or rather a kind of insouciance, was an absolute requirement.

We had glimpses of wilder flights. Even the flamboyant sophomores recounted with awe the exploits of a seldom-seen, half-legendary barracks figure, a former Golden Gloves boxer and very active cocksman (now there's an early 1950s period term!). Nobody else had even thought of sneaking a girl into his room for immoral or any other purposes. He had not only done so but, when Father McCallin was alerted by her cries of passion and tried to catch the guilty parties, the guilty male party had the presence of mind to bang open his back window and, when Father Mac hurried around to investigate, to hustle the girl out the door. On another occasion, he had supposedly returned, the front of his trousers covered with blood, complaining, "Son of a bitch! She didn't *tell* me she was a virgin!" He was also supposed to be incredibly intelligent and to have a fund of arcane information. He did make up this epigram, using the author of our text on Thomistic psychology,

> Man has an intellect, that we know,
> For George P. Klubertanz tells us so.

It didn't seem possible to rise to this level—a solo act that attracted without seeking approval, and that required more knowledge and daring than most of us had. It wasn't always easy to emulate even the less intellectual feats of the sophomores. Still, it was a lot easier and more immediately gratifying than studying.

Besides, studying was a lonely activity, and as far as possible, we did everything in a group. Our first venture indicated that this might not always be a good idea. Released from the first day of official orientation, we reinforced each others' collective idiocy and walked the seventeen blocks to the College of St. Teresa, known as CST, the Catholic girls' school, to see if we could meet some girls. Instead, we encountered a super-dreadnought nun who thundered, "Take your cars and yourselves and *go!*" We didn't have any cars, but we went, and when the incident was mentioned unfavorably during the next day's orientation, we tried not to slide down too far in our chairs. But CST had officially sanctioned means, called mixers, of getting girls together with boys, and we attended those in a group, and when some of us got fixed up with blind dates, it was generally in pairs or trios.

We made more consistent attempts to get to know each other. One of us would invite the group to visit our hometown. This covered a wide spectrum, from a day trip to the Mucken-thaler farmhouse in Kansas to a weekend in St. Louis where we were shown the wonders of real civilization. I was less puzzled or awed than I was supposed to be because I knew something about farms and enough about cities not to betray amazement to people who expected it of me.

In Boonville, though I was on home ground, I was highly sensitive to my friends' perspective. They had been amused at my accent and at the size of my hometown—they didn't tease Florian Muckenthaler because he had sense enough to be modest without needing to be; and while I knew that my dialect and point of origin didn't measure up to big-city standards, I was a little hostile toward the people who criticized them. We got off the bus. I suggested, with calculated hesitation, that we *could* get a cab.

A town this size *had* cabs? Amazing! But how far could it be to your house?

Well, I said, we could walk, and we set off. My house was nearly two miles away, down one steep hill and up another, longer one, beyond city streets to a road flanked by a cemetery and a field across which we could see the Missouri Training School for Boys, and up what was obviously a country road dotted with mailboxes. By the time we got to my house, they had decided that Boonville was not all that small. And they were impressed by the animals because none of them had ever seen a cow up close. One of them asked, "Can I touch it?"

They were less impressed by the farm boy from my high school graduating class who joined us on a bar-hopping expedition to Columbia. Looking back, I should have asked another friend, who was already cooler than all four of us put together would ever be, but he was still in high school and anyway I didn't think of it. The farm boy was very shrewd, but he lacked the signs of polish that would have impressed my new friends, and the fact that he vomited out the back window on the way home made him seem a hopeless rube. It depended on who did it, and where, I suppose.

But when it was time to leave for Kansas City, my companions gratefully accepted the offer of a ride to the bus station. After we got back, they still teased me—for what I did and said, not for what I was. That stung, but I could see that it was not unfair.

Nobody teased the Puerto Rican because he comported himself more circumspectly and was not provincial. It wasn't practical to visit his hometown, but some of us did go with him to the Mexican community on the west side of Kansas City where he bought records and other reminders of his first language. Some of us were taking first-year Spanish, but we knew nothing about the customs and culture and very little of the language we heard—which, our friend assured us, was not real Spanish anyway, so we needn't feel guilty. Once we went to Sunday mass with him, which was still in Latin. We managed well enough until we got to the sermon. The priest was quite impassioned, but about what we didn't know. When we left, we asked our friend what the sermon was about. Lust, he said. We gathered that the preacher was against it.

Most of us didn't know much more about basketball than we did about Spanish, but five of us showed up when the Rockhurst College basketball team had open tryouts. Only the Kentuckian and I had played on high school teams, and after the first few days we were the only barracks boys still going to practice. I was at a disadvantage because my high school coach had made rare and perfunctory attempts to teach us anything. Once he had tried to run us through a set play, and it was so insanely complicated that even without defensive players on the court we kept crashing into each other. In any case, most of the gyms we played in were so small (at Clarksburg, the out-of-bounds line was the wall) that there wasn't room to maneuver on offense, and when the other team had the ball, a zone defense was the only way to avoid gridlock. The Rockhurst coach ran a highly controlled offense and a man-to-man defense, so I was at a considerable disadvantage. And though at six foot one inch (in shoes) I had been one of the tallest centers in my league, even I could see that I was going to have to try a new act, so I announced that I was a guard. Facing the basket, I could see what was going on even if I didn't always understand it.

This venture into college athletics seems insane by modern standards, but the Kentuckian and I lasted until the final cut and either of us was better than at least one of the freshmen retained because he was on scholarship. He was good at standing around in one spot, and even better, during the season, at sitting in one spot. But even at tip-off, Rockhurst was playing students, most of whom, when Rockhurst got a new coach, greatly improved the quality of play in intramurals. Only Bob Williams of the starting five would certainly have made even a small college team today, and he looked and moved more like a high school football lineman than a basketball player. But he could score in an amazing variety of ways, and as I discovered, he could play defense, too.

Well into practice, I realized that I was probably not going to make the squad and that even if I did I would have a marginal role. I had enjoyed the one-on-one and fast break drills, but the deliberate style of play confused almost as much as it bored me. So in one scrimmage I opened up, cut through the first-team defense, and scored three or four baskets that looked completely out of control and probably were. I was enjoying myself enormously. The coach was not. "Can't anybody stop him?" he shouted. Bob Williams took the assignment and not only didn't I touch the ball again, I spent a good deal of time on my ass.

When the squad was chosen, the Kentuckian and I each commiserated over the injustice of the other's not being selected, but I was not really disappointed. With the rest of the barracks group, we formed an intramural team that had no plays and spotty talent. My friend was a good post man, so I was free to shoot from outside and for the first time scored twenty points in a game.

Besides, basketball practice took up a lot of time, which could be devoted to other extracurricular activities. Sex, drugs, and rock and roll were not available to us. Even thinking about sex was for Catholics a mortal sin, and occupied most of the time I spent in confession. Rock and roll had not been invented, and rhythm and blues had not penetrated the popular gloop that filled the ears of most people of our race and class. Nicotine was not regarded as a drug, and it seemed—at least to me— slightly nerdish not to smoke. Drugs were for Negroes, jazz musicians (especially drummers), and Robert Mitchum. Like most of my generation, I still have trouble thinking of alcohol as a drug.

Free time, some that should have been spent in class or studying, involved attempts to buy beer while under twenty-one, the legal age in Missouri. In Kansas, the legal age was eighteen, which accounted for a good deal of traffic between Rockhurst and Leo's Blatz Tavern across the line; and while I wouldn't reach eighteen for another year, I had no trouble there and only sporadically east of State Line Road. Once we set out with the highly ambitious goal of having a beer in every bar on State Street in Kansas City, Kansas, and very nearly did.

When the upperclassmen got to know us a little better, they began to include us in some of their expeditions. Most commonly these were keg parties held in special preserves at Swope Park. Someone would pick up the keg; someone else would bring a minimal amount of food; someone always brought a sleeve of paper cups; experienced drinkers brought quart mason jars. No one tapped kegs often enough to be really confident, so the insertion of the pump was always watched nervously, and then we had to drink a good deal of foam before we got much liquid. I don't think we ever finished a keg—sixteen gallons was the smallest in those days—but on the principle of waste not, want not, even normally respectable residents of the barracks stayed as close to the keg as they could for as long as they could. I don't know how drunk we got, though to the sober burghers we were undoubtedly obnoxious. Fortunately, Swope Park is very large.

At another kind of party you could get drunk and obnoxious without being noticed. Some of our mentors had names like Moloney, O'Shea, Growney, and Coffey, and they introduced us to the dances given by the Irish-American Social Club and its parent organization, the Royal and Ancient Order of Hibernians. These were impressive even by barracks standards. At one dance, the first girl passed out before the band started playing. At another, a couple of bouncers quite mildly requested that while having a girl slung over my shoulder was perfectly acceptable, standing on a table approached the prevailing bounds of decorum. By this time, I think, I was an upperclassman; and although the bouncers seemed a bit stuffy, they had asked nicely, so I got down. I have no idea who the girl was or what happened to her. I doubt that she did either.

But keg parties and Hibernian revelry were rare events in our social calendar. As we got older, we drank less, if not more legally. Actually, my contemporaries were far more sober than

Raw Material

I. Perhaps I eventually learned something from waking up with every joint hurting or being unable to find my glasses. Perhaps I realized, more through observation of others than through direct experience, that vomiting is not one of the chief marks of sophistication.

Besides, some of the worst examples left Rockhurst and the barracks after my sophomore year, and I was not interested in becoming a bad, or horrible, example to the newcomers.

Today the authorities might worry about our drinking excessively and illegally and offer counseling—I could see even then that a couple of the sophomores obviously needed it—but my parents' generation had grown up with prohibition and regarded evasion of liquor laws as normal. The only sartorial advice Father McCallin ever gave—in those days priests didn't have to worry about what to wear—was to buy an overcoat with an internal pocket large enough to hold a fifth of whiskey. Like most Jesuits, he made clear distinctions between illegality and immorality. He was anything but latitudinarian in matters of sexual morality and thought rhythm and blues suitable only for African fertility rites, but he once defined theological drunkenness as being passed out on the floor with no one to help you to bed. Some of us, a bit more scrupulous, confessed the sin of drunkenness when we passed out or, more frequently at first, threw up. Those of us who kept practicing learned to get rid of the beer by the more usual method, and it seems fitting that the best-known Rockhurst alumnus is George Wendt, who played Norm on "Cheers."

Not everybody in our group wanted to be a great drinker or a wild success with women or an outstanding student or athlete or, God knows, the well-rounded man that our liberal education was supposed to produce. In fact, by setting its own modest standards, the group protected us from having to meet any real challenges.

Having dealt with college students for more than forty years, I can see that this huddling together is an inevitable part of the process of encountering a new world. But the sooner it ends, the better. As the conventionally successful Oxford man says in Evelyn Waugh's *Brideshead Revisited*, "You'll find you spend half of your second year shaking off the undesirable friends you made in your first."

The undesirable acquaintance I had to shake was my persona. The Jesuit idea of the Whole Man didn't have much appeal for me, but about this time I read Aldous Huxley's *Antic Hay*, with its image of the Compleat Man, an imposture devised by the mild hero who puts on a false beard and a coat with padded shoulders and acquires an image that sounds like a blend of Friedrich Nietzsche and François Rabelais. I had never heard of these writers, but Theodore Gumbril seemed to be enjoying himself without expending much effort, and that seemed to me ideal.

Perhaps the comfortable little world of the barracks had begun to seem restrictive. I was more interested in reading for its own sake than were any of my friends. Somehow I wound up in a drama class and spent much of my spring semester in rehearsals. I was even more conventionally religious than all but the man who left for the seminary after that year. I had the sense that I was different, and I wanted to stand out.

Some of my efforts were ludicrous in execution and painful in memory. I didn't have the stomach to be a mighty drinker or the obvious attractions to be a ladies man, so I tried for versatility, at least in the very tame versions of tales about my past imitated from the family saga and Grandpa Murray's outrageous stories. Some of the upperclassmen thought I was serious—perhaps to some degree I was—and made me feel so ridiculous that I gradually began the process of abandoning the behavior I was unconsciously parodying.

As for getting rid of other friends, that process took care of itself. The Kentuckian did not return for the second semester, and my roommate moved into the place he vacated in the lower barracks, perhaps to get out from under Father McCallin's watchful eye and perhaps to get away from me. If the first was his motive, it didn't work: near the end of the second semester, he and another member of the group ran into Father McCallin while carrying open cans of beer and, after a painful hearing, were expelled.

I never got caught for that, but I missed a great many curfews and in other respects made a nuisance of myself. Before I could leave the barracks at the end of my freshman year, I recited "The Hound of Heaven" to expiate my latest offense. Father McCallin listened to it and dismissed me without further comment. But near the end of the summer, my father asked me if I wanted to live off campus. I told him no, largely because, without any social or academic base, I would have felt completely isolated. The question seemed very uncharacteristic of him, and I wondered why he had asked, though natural disinclination of a growing son to talk to a father longer than necessary prevented me from discussing his motive. When I returned to Rockhurst in September 1952, I learned from the associate dean that I was on disciplinary probation for repeated violation of barracks rules, and further offenses would result in my being told to move out.

This did not seem a serious threat. As far as we had been able to determine, the only rules for sophomores and up were (1) do not pass out in front of Father McCallin's door and block his egress, and (2) do not allow your mail to overflow your mailbox and create litter. I managed to live with these and any other rules for three more years, partly because I got very little mail; partly because two members of my group had left and the third dropped out after the fall term of our sophomore year.

Coincidentally or not, I made the honor roll for the first time the following spring. Moreover, the flamboyant upperclassmen had become object lessons rather than role models: the heavy drinkers were in obvious trouble and the man who had sauntered out to the girl's car had impregnated and married her and moved across the baseball field to the married students' apartments.

Left to consider my own tastes and talents, I began to spend more time following them and less time with people merely because they were handy. Subsequent roommates had less influence on me—except for the one with whom I had least in common, for he introduced me to rhythm and blues. I made friends with some of the natives. But they went home at night. It wasn't possible to do things with them on impulse, like go to a movie or grab a beer or go down to the field house for a pickup basketball game in the evening. So while the male bonds became looser and less restrictive, the barracks (and, after they were torn down, Dowling House on the far corner of the campus) remained the center of the day-to-day life that had nothing particular to do with education or the intellect or getting me wherever it was I thought I wanted to go.

Healthy Boy-Girl Relationships:

A Distraction

Of course, "co-ed glamour" is not present—but you are not going to college to major in entertainment.

—Rockhurst College brochure

While Rockhurst did not admit women as students, the Jesuits were forced, grudgingly, to acknowledge that they existed. Nothing in the advertising said anything about vows of celibacy, and in fact all freshmen were required to take a course called Catholic Marriage. Therefore, if we were to establish "healthy boy-girl relationships," in the often-parodied terminology of the time, young Catholic women had to be available to save us from the wiles of heretics and heathens.

Thus, at the same time that the Jesuits promised to shield us from coed glamor, they equivocated. Next to the question about training by and with men in one brochure is a picture of students inspecting sides of beef in a meat packing plant. But just above it is another captioned "Speakers' Seminar over Station KCKN," with two undeniable women in the center of the group. They were a necessary evil if Rockhurst was going to have a mixed chorus or pep club or, since nobody would have been willing or allowed to appear in drag, produce most plays.

Therefore, the wisdom of the church had seen to it that Catholic men's colleges should be located at not-impossible distances from Catholic women's colleges: Loyola and Marymount in Los Angeles, Loyola and Mundelein in Chicago, the College of St. Benedict's and Mount Saint Scholastica in Atchinson, and, seventeen blocks from the gate of the Rockhurst barracks, the College of St. Teresa, named after Saint Teresa of Avila, the patron of headaches.

CST, as Rockhurst's counterpart was generally called, had a perfectly respectable academic program. There was considerable duplication in the liberal arts curricula of the two colleges, but the preprofessional programs were gender stereotyped. CST had links to the Catholic nursing schools for girls who wanted a B.S. in nursing; Rockhurst had links to the engineering programs at St. Louis University and Marquette. The science program at CST was so rudimentary that Rockhurst admitted one woman who showed great promise in that field. God knows what hand-wringing and soul-searching preceded that decision.

But as even the CST *Teresian* admitted somewhat ruefully, the M.R.S. degree was the real goal of many of its students. "Alumnae News" consisted mostly of engagements, marriages, and the inevitable birth announcements, some following soon enough to occasion finger counting if not pointing. One headline read "Boo Turner First Senior to Marry," and a later roundup of Christmastime engagements concluded, "It has been suggested that the *Teresian* would save time by simply publishing the names of students *not* engaged." It probably would have. On average, 43 percent of American Catholic women's college students married during this period; 85 to 90 percent of CST students did.

Not all CST students were reconciled to marriage. One columnist, though admitting that "we are the marrying grads," maintained that the single woman "knows where she is going, and she'll find the road much smoother without a man who would probably be more of a burden than a boon." Brave words for 1952—especially in a paper that the previous term had denounced the *Ladies' Home Journal* for wanting to free "womanhood from the 'shackles of an outworn, outdated moral code.' " But this writer was ahead of her time: her column was countered by the headline "College Plans Brides' Course for June 23–27," and "Father Lyons Asks Girls to Attend Marriage Lectures" at meetings of the "Social Hygiene Society."

Even those not driven by these lectures to the vocation of the single life (the language used at the time) had their doubts. One humor column included the following dialog:

> "Fr. Freeman [a Rockhurst professor notorious for encouraging healthy boy-girl relationships] says we should marry somebody better than ourselves."
> "So what?"
> "So nobody gets married."

In contrast, a headline from the *Teresian* read, "First Mixer Success; Men Outnumber Women."

The schizophrenia about printable aspects of male-female encounters was even stronger in attitudes toward romance, sex, and morality. Romance was entirely secular, and as now, was largely defined by popular culture. For example, in September 1951, Nat King Cole's version of "Too Young" was still near the top of *Variety's* charts for sheet music, disc jockey requests, and juke-box plays for the twenty-second week and had just become the number one hit in England. The only song in the top forty-six addressed specifically to teenagers, its lyrics stated plaintively, if ungrammatically, "They try to tell us we're too young, too young to really be in love." No one remarked on the irony that the sentiments were expressed by someone who was already over thirty because the phenomenon of the teenage idol on screen and record had not arrived. As a high school student, I rather liked the tune but thought the words nonsense because, though often horny, I had never really thought I was in love.

Not long after I matriculated, the song "Tenderly" became a hit in a number of versions. By this time, I was ready to think that I was in love, and the lyrics defined and perhaps prompted the emotion. After forty-two years, I (and almost everyone else born in the 1930s) can quote them from memory.

People raised on the music of the 1960s (such as "Why Don't We Do It in the Road") would probably think the words of the song hopelessly lame. The only noise, human or natural, is muted. No heavy breathing or moaning. No body fluids. There is moisture, but it is only mist.

"Tenderly" sounds innocent enough now, but in 1951 it implied at least an occasion, if not a near occasion, of sin. Romance might lead to sex, and Catholics were taught that sex outside of marriage was a sin. In fact, the course in Catholic Marriage dealt primarily with whom we couldn't marry and why not. The only mention of the physical side of marriage occurred in a discussion of why the rhythm method of birth control was permissible: "After all, one is not required to have sexual intercourse at any particular time."

This was not very informative, but it was, by design, not inflammatory. Unmarried people were forbidden to indulge in sexual intercourse or any other means of physical gratification. A chaste and affectionate kiss might be just barely within permissible bounds. A kiss that anyone enjoyed was suspect; French kissing was a ticket to hell. Anything beyond that was express. The question on everyone's mind, as David Lodge acknowledged when he used it as the title of his 1980 novel, was *How Far Can You Go?*

It had something to do with reality; the ideal was better expressed in Paul Claudel's play *The Tidings Brought to Mary,* produced at the College of St. Teresa in the spring of 1952 as "a CST contribution to the plea for world peace and freedom as expressed through the theatre." I don't know if the play had as much effect as the Rosary Crusade, which an editorial called a more powerful weapon than the atomic bomb in melting the Iron Curtain, but the subsequent review called it "by far the most superior play we've had here."

Forty years later, I was pleased to see the review, for I had my last speaking part in a play as a medieval French architect, Pierre de Craon, previously and subsequently virginal, who has laid lustful hands on Violaine before the play begins. As punishment, he is immediately stricken with leprosy. Out of forgiveness as well as happiness at her impending marriage to another man, Violaine gives him a kiss that cures him, removes female power over his soul, and gives him "freedom and dismissal from this life." It also causes her to become leprous, so that instead of a useful millstone paired with another, she becomes the capital stone of the cathedral at Rhiems, which Pierre, free from sensual distractions, goes on to build. Between those events, she becomes a recluse, performs a miracle that restores her sister's child to life, and dies in a burst of rhetoric, plainchant, and church bells on the premise that "Man is the priest, but it is not forbidden to woman to be victim."

A lot of other stuff goes on, but since Pierre disappears for a hundred pages after the prologue, and I spent most of the interval smoking in the wings, I didn't realize that until recently, when I read the whole play for the first time. But even then it was clear that sex was very dangerous and exciting, that women were supposed to control the situation, and that they suffered the more if they didn't.

If one simple kiss could get you into that kind of trouble, imagine what more serious kinds of activity could lead to. Some of us took this moral theology more seriously than others, but even those who had motive, the knowledge of methods, and the confidence that they would live until their next confession had, in secular terms, been conditioned to think less of physical than emotional gratification, to fall in love with love (as a much older song put it) rather than fall into bed.

And to fall into bed, you had to find a bed. In the early 1950s, that wasn't impossible, but it was hard for most of us to imagine. Even married couples had twin beds, at least in the movies. Desk clerks supposedly checked wedding rings, and that would be embarrassing. If they didn't, then the place obviously catered not to romance but to lust, and we weren't ready for that. Besides, it would look funny going to a motel not merely without luggage—I had the leather suitcase but had imprudently stuck a Rockhurst pennant on the side—but without a car.

Cars were supposed to provide maximum opportunity, but to an anxious virgin six feet tall the logistics seemed impossible to imagine even with enthusiastic cooperation. Anyway, I didn't have a car. Drive-in movies were known as passion pits, but to those with performance anxiety or guilt about trying to perform at all, there wasn't much more than a little nuzzling and fumbling.

The horns of the dilemma—or the dilemmas of horniness—were particularly acute because young men were either frustrated or guilty. This led to ambivalent attitudes about females as, on the one hand, prick-teasers, and, on the other, loose women, better known as sluts. Either way, males felt resentful. No one I knew had heard of the term "sadomasochism," but those who responded to Mickey Spillane's novels, which began to appear in the late 1940s (very surreptitiously in the barracks), had a working definition. Spillane tapped into the simultaneous desire for and fear of women. Mike Hammer could penetrate a woman with penis or bullet or both and enjoy it all.

The only copy of a Spillane novel I can now find in local public libraries is a large-print edition—life is not unironic—of *Vengeance Is Mine*. This novel reveals on the last page that the temptress/murderess is in fact a man and therefore trebly liable to execution. Otherwise, it is standard fare: a very desirable woman slugs Hammer because he won't "make" her; Hammer hits her

> across the mouth as hard as he could. Her head rocked, but she still stood there, and now her eyes were more vicious than ever. "Still want me to make you?"
> "Make me," she said.

Later he is challenged by another woman:

> Demanding that I come to her. . .and rip that damn robe right off her back and see what it was that went to make up the flesh of a goddess. For one second my face must have changed and she thought I was going to do it, because her eyes went wide and I saw her shoulders twitch and this time there was woman-fear behind the desire and she was a mortal for an instant, a female crouching away from the male.

As far as I was concerned, all of this was pure fantasy. I may have heard of rape, but I could not imagine anyone committing it. My desires were far gentler and not very specific.

We had a rudimentary vocabulary for the sexual activity we could imagine. "Necking"—a quaint period term—meant just that: neck and above. In secular, indeed vulgar, terms, that was first base. The baseball metaphor continued around the bases, though I don't remember that "scoring" had come into the language at that time. Any physical activity was known as "making out." One classmate, a caricature of the prurient adolescent male, would ask me every Monday, "Didja make out last weekend? Didja?" This continued until I told him the longest version I knew of the shaggy dog story about a woman's promise to give a man a sleeve job after the wedding. When I delivered the punch line—"So he covered himself with vaseline, slipped on the floor, hit his head on the bathtub, and died"—he looked at me in silence, turned and walked away, and never spoke to me again.

I felt justified because, while it was perfectly normal to be interested in girls, it was generally regarded as not cool to boast and even worse to ask. In the barracks, we rarely talked in those terms because it wasn't safe to joke about other people's girls. When a friend went to Union Station to see his girlfrient off on a trip, I quoted Frankie Laine's line in "Jealousy," "My peace departs." He did not find the pun amusing. For the most part, we respected each others' sentiments because some of us shared them. We wanted very badly to be in love, and there was a lot of lying on bunks, romantic sighs the only emissions. Our colleagues went on with normal life.

Of course, it helped to have a romantic object. My roommate had a girlfriend back home, which left him a lot of time. The rest of us had to find local girls.

In fact, we didn't have to find girls: they found us. I don't remember who made the arrangements—probably the girl-friend of a local boy one of us had met in class—but some of us were invited to a party at a girl's house with an equal number of CST students (known as "Tessies") who had gone to St. Teresa's High School. I don't remember how long it took us to pair off, but I do know that the males did not get to choose. I was not at all displeased: the girl was slim and in my view the most elegant of her group. She looked and smelled different from Boonville girls.

I had learned how to dance—slowly, and mostly backward—because that was the only sure-fire way to get close to a girl, though at high school dances and even college mixers the nuns insisted on being able to see light between the bodies. Things were more up-to-date in Kansas City than I expected. This girl adjusted my left hand—they did things differently there—and moved toward me. Close was redefined. As the phrase went, if she had been any closer, she'd have been behind me. "Tenderly" might not have been the first 45 RPM record we danced to, but it wasn't long before it dropped onto the stack.

That settled it: I was in love. For several months I called her almost daily; saw her, in the company of one or two couples, most weekends; made an ass of myself; and enjoyed every moment. I can't remember a thing she said—for that matter, I can't remember anything I said, which means I must not have had any good lines—but I am reminded of her every time I hear the opening lines of the Eagles' song "Lying Eyes": "City girls just seem to find out early / How to open doors with just a smile." She wasn't lying, and she wasn't manipulative, but she was definitely in control. That was ok; I had been taught that girls were supposed to be in control, physically and emotionally, of these situations. When, after several months, I asked her to go steady, she refused, and we broke up.

Perhaps this sort of thing wasn't as serious as I had thought. The only thing that really bothered me was that I didn't have a girlfriend. I missed what would now seem very minor physical gratification; I missed even more having an outlet for affection.

But it was near Christmas. One fringe benefit of the academic calendar is the regular punctuation of the year by vacations, semesters, and summer breaks, all very useful for getting over or out of emotional entanglements, especially if you leave town.

It was time to look for a new girl. Again, that wasn't hard, because the College of St. Teresa and the nursing schools attached to Catholic hospitals all sponsored mixers. Rockhurst had dances instead—some, fairly formal (suits and ties) in the field house; at least one, informal, in the war surplus cafeteria.

After forty years, the words may have changed, but the song remains the same: What's your major (except for nurses); where are you from; do you like this music; seen any good movies; do you know the girl dancing with my friend? Phone numbers—hers, never yours. Awkward pauses. Even more awkward attempts to impress. I don't remember dating anyone I first encountered at a mixer, though one man a couple of classes behind me actually married a girl he met at one.

Looking back, it is easy to be cynical about these things. It's hard not to be, and in my senior year, I got a great deal of pleasure out of reading in the CST newspaper some helpful hints about how to meet and if necessary get rid of men at mixers. Since by that time I was a regular columnist and co-editor of the Rockhurst paper and could print anything the moderator didn't talk us out of, I wrote some tips on how to get rid of women. It seemed funny at the time, and it isn't quite as bad as some of the things I wrote; it had at least some basis in experience.

Mostly we depended on blind dates. Like arranged marriages in older cultures, these worked surprisingly well, probably because the person responsible usually doubled or tripled and thus had to be fairly careful. I met some nice women that way. Some of them were too nice—mostly nurses, who were more conservative than the Tessies and kept absurd hours, though only one, when I took her back to the hospital, wanted to round off the date with a visit to the hospital chapel. She was pretty and serious in a way I had found attractive, but that was not my ideal scenario for the end of an evening. If she was struggling against impulses similar to mine—this occurs to me forty years late—she had found the ideal means. I liked her anyway and continued to see her occasionally until I left Kansas City. The last time I called, her sister informed me that she was engaged. I hope it worked out.

By the time I was released to summer in Boonville, my social life was about the same as my grade point average—a little above average. I don't remember dating that summer. I was working nine-hour days lifting hundred-pound feed sacks, playing softball, and drinking with local friends, mostly the ones who were going to college or about to. These were good ways to sublimate. Besides, the girls I knew at home seemed too young or too familiar or too provincial or all three, and I had spent a good deal of effort trying to cut old ties and didn't want any new ones. So my sophomore year started with an empty dance card.

But then I had a lot more contacts, and the remaining member of my original group had temporary access to a car. Before long, someone arranged blind dates with some freshmen boarding students at CST. This was a group with whom I had no previous experience. They were not exactly kept in purdah, but they did not seem grateful about the absence of veils. When they entertained callers in the lounge, rumor had it, every couple had to have at least two feet on the floor, preferably one each, at all times. Since the lounge was across the hall from and in easy view of the reception desk, staffed by the most forbidding nuns in the community, any public display of affection was unlikely: the lounge was more like a cold shower than a hot tub.

Some of the boarding students chafed at these restrictions
and voiced their frustrations in the unofficial College of St.
Teresa marching song, to the tune of "The Washington and Lee
Swing":

We are the girls of CST.
There's not a man in this damned nunnery.
And every night at eight they bar the door,
I don't know what the hell I e-ver came here for.
And when I'm on the train and homeward bound,
I'm gonna turn that town right upside down,
I'm gonna drink and smoke and neck by heck,
    yes, by heck,
Away from CST.

This implication of self-assertion under repression was
borne out in practice. As usual, the pairing off had already been
done by whoever fixed us up. Our dates were from the same
Missouri town, larger than Boonville and smaller than St. Louis.
The driver's date was blondeish, not very tall, and Germanic
(which was suitable for him), and looked very self-contained
(which was not). Mine—call her K.—was taller, Irish in coloring
and openness. I don't remember who the third couple was, but
there were six people in the car. Since I was the largest male,
K. sat on my lap, and she made the obligatory Tessie joke about
forgetting to bring the convent-recommended magazine, or was
it a phone book, to insert between us. The contact was less
inflammatory than the nuns imagined, if they did or could
imagine it. The insulating magazine may belong to the same
mythic realm as the deadly reflecting patent leather shoes that
supposedly allowed lustful males a glimpse of lingerie.

Instead, I saw *The Snows of Kilimanjaro* from the top balcony
of an enormous, ornate, first-run theater. I remember our location

because, in one shot of a bullfight from the last row of seats, we were doubly distanced from the action.

Those who have read Hemingway's story but have not seen the movie would be justifiably puzzled because there isn't any bullfighting in the story, nor any Spanish Civil War, nor any episode about Harry living decadently and writing badly on the Riviera, nor any girl in Paris, nor any real airplane to take Harry to a hospital instead of to the white oblivion or immortality at the top of Mount Kilimanjaro.

Years later, I had forgotten almost everything about the movie except the long shot of the bull ring and Ava Gardner, who couldn't act much but seemed to me far sexier than any blonde before or after. So I checked out a videotape to refresh my memory. The long shot didn't come out quite the same, but Ava Gardner looked as good as ever, and the subtext of the movie—along with my memory of what I was like at eighteen—helped me understand why the love affair with this new girl was doomed from the start.

Some of the movie's messages were too subtle for me to understand consciously at the time: it's ok to be a real jerk if you are a writer; if you lose Ava Gardner, Susan Hayward will turn up and be a lot better companion on safari. Also, unless you have broader shoulders than Gregory Peck, don't wear a safari jacket.

But the chief line of reasoning was clear even then: going places is essential to a writer, but women prevent you from going places. The conclusion is obvious. I didn't take a course in logic until the next semester—only A I got in twenty-seven hours of philosophy and religion—but I could follow a line of reasoning. Moreover, I had heard Father McCallin talk with the most scarifying pity about a married scholar prevented by domestic cares from exercising his vocation. Of course, Father McCallin also warned against marrying an intellectual woman because she would stack the dishes in the sink and read a book. (I did, and she did.) It's not that he was the worst male chauvinist at Rockhurst, though he articulated most clearly the philosophy implied in much of our education and stated overtly in the brochure: women represented not just a moral danger—even a secular priest could tell you that—but an intellectual distraction even if you did what everyone was supposed to do and got married.

I was willing enough to be distracted, and for the moment my morals were safe enough, and I had no desire to be a virginal church architect like Pierre in *The Tidings Brought to Mary*, but I did want to be a writer, or at least a newspaperman, and I wanted to go places. The girl beside me was cast, though it took me three years to act on and forty to realize, in the unenviable role of the girl who gets dumped in Hemingway's "The End of Something," which had also gotten spliced into *The Snows of Kilimanjaro*.

My classmate was obviously smitten, and for a few weeks I was just along for the ride. Not an unpleasant one, for K. had a sense of humor, which seemed rare for a girl in those days, and a directness that I had encountered in few men and no women at all outside my immediate family.

One night, as we pulled into the parking lot of a bar across the Kansas line, K. looked in her compact mirror and said, "My lipstick is smeared."

"Well," I said wittily, "that's not my fault."

She looked straight at me and said, in a way that was both withering and provocative, "Yes. I know."

I didn't have to be Cary Grant—fortunately—to recognize that kind of cue. The lipstick got smeared, and over the next three years we smeared enough to cover a good-sized wall.

We had been told repeatedly by nuns and priests that double-dating was morally preferable because the presence of others inhibited passion. Unlike the advice about patent leather shoes, this turned out to be true. When the Teutonic pair broke up and left us alone, things heated up.

Comparisons are invidious and might make trouble, so I won't say that K. was the best kisser I have encountered, but she was the first really good one. (There were, in my limited experience, no bad ones.) Catholic girls stayed longer at that stage because everything beyond kissing, and even the messier stages of that, were forbidden. K. had learned an open-mouthed style, called wind kissing, which could go on, theoretically, until one partner passed out from carbon dioxide and, practically, until everything tingled. This and some of the other things we did remind me of the little boy who comes home with a bean up his nose. His mother asks, "Why on earth did you do that?" "You never told me not to," he answers. French kissing was out; no priest or nun had mentioned wind kissing.

Of course, most of the things K. and I did were covered under the general guidelines, but as we got more experienced and bolder we did a lot of other things they had specifically told us not to do. As frequently happens, one thing led to another—behind almost every bush on the CST grounds; in back seats in Loose Memorial (known as Loose Morals) Park; in movie theaters. When we visited each other's homes, she came to my bedroom; I don't say it would never have occurred to me to go to hers, but I was too chicken. I suppose this could be called foreplay though, to put it delicately, no one ever swung the club. Still, we did as much sweating in confessionals as we did in the bushes. Once, returning to the barracks at dawn after a particularly frustrating night in the back seat of a car in Swope Park (with an armed, off-duty cop and his date in the front seat), I longed for the peace and security of a Jesuit seminary. A few hours' sleep was enough to dispel that idea.

In a way, the emotional intimacy was more exciting and far less frustrating than the physical because we didn't have to hold back. She was the first girl I ever saw without makeup, and I didn't think she looked nearly as bad as she claimed to think. She was the first woman—the only one—I allowed to pluck my eyebrows, and she showed me that a hairpin pulled across the skin was a good way to get rid of the nest of blackheads on either side of my nose.

She told me the first risqué story I ever heard from a Catholic girl, about someone overhearing Cockney newlyweds through a thin hotel wall. The woman repeats, at intervals, with increasing emphasis on the second word, " 'Ow 'bout it, Charlie?" Finally Charlie answers, " 'Ow 'bout what?" " 'Ow 'bout gettin' *off?*" I was too inexperienced to know that this was an unlikely problem.

I was equally ill informed about other matters. One night K. complained of not feeling well. "I hope it's not catching," I said. "I hardly think so," she said. Long pause. "Oh." This was the first time I had heard a girl refer even this obliquely to menstruation. Another time, discussing an upcoming dance, she asked if I minded if she wore falsies—they were necessary to make her dress fit. I agreed, and after the dance, to which we rode with a Jesuit's nephew, she pulled them out and sighed in comfort. The driver, inhibited even by my standards, nearly drove up a lamp post.

We became intimate enough to negotiate. Once I entered a beard-growing contest at Rockhurst, and after the finals, in which I finished well out of the running, she asked me to shave. I agreed to do so—but only if she would lose five pounds.

By this time we were well beyond the dewy-eyed romantic stage where "Tenderly" could serve as background music. In fact I don't connect any songs with K. (Once K. and I were at the Kansas City Municipal Airport and I caught a glimpse of my first girlfriend, dressed very fashionably. She looked good, but I did not feel nostalgic.) We occasionally danced, but we no longer needed that excuse for physical contact.

We also spent a lot of time talking. Much of this was over the phone because all boarding students at CST were confined to campus during the week. But we also talked during our time together on weekends—a good thing, because I would have exploded from frustration. We didn't talk about books or ideas—years later she characterized herself accurately as intelligent but not intellectual.

Another movie revealed the depth of the disparity in our tastes. We had gotten back together after one of our periodic separations, but one night we had a serious argument about which movie we were going to see. This was unusual, because normally, as long as the theater was dark and not too crowded, we didn't care what was showing. But this time she wanted to go to a current hit; I was far more interested in *New Faces* (based on the revue that introduced Eartha Kitt, Ronnie Graham, Alice Ghostley, and Robert Clary, among others). I refused to compromise, and afterward she admitted that she had enjoyed the movie. But I resented having to insist.

This kind of disagreement was uncommon in the early stages. Mostly we liked to do the same things, and we talked frankly about our families and our friends. I learned a good deal from her about openness and generosity.

Not enough, perhaps. One thing we—I—never talked about was the future. While I had no particular idea what I was going to do with my life, I had a general premonition that the image of domesticity prevalent at the time wouldn't have much part in it. From about 1968 on, the solution would have been simple—move in together off campus. But in the first half of the 1950s that was unimaginable even in social terms. And in the moral terms we had been given, there were only two alternatives that I could see: break up or marry. I could not imagine the second.

It took a long and painful time to choose the first alternative, or rather to stick to the decision once I had made it. It was always my idea. I have since realized that my position was in a way more uncomfortable than hers because while she felt pain at the loss, I felt some pain and a good deal of guilt. And if guilt had been graded, my undergraduate transcript would have been much more impressive than the one on file. But I hesitated to break up with her because I felt that she was an unusual person, because she was physically the most exciting woman I had known, and because I both desired and feared what she had to offer in the long run. I suspected that I could be comfortable, even happy, with her. I also knew that I would stop moving.

So I did break up with her. By this time I had got over being awed by girls, but I was still afraid of them, and I adopted the cynical view that they wanted to exploit men by marrying them or reforming them or using them in other ways. Some of the columns I wrote during my senior year sound sexist today, but they were rooted not in a sense of superiority to or fear of women but in a distrust of my own natural impulses to seek support and comfort in domesticity.

Fortunately or not, there was the spiritual outlet. By this time, I had a confessor. Going to confession anonymously, behind a screen, produced stress, but all you got was a penance (we used to compare and joke about the severity), absolution, and the injunction to go and sin no more. If you got the right priest, as comedian George Carlin put it, you were back on the street in five minutes. Having a regular confessor meant telling your sins barefaced to a priest who knew what you had confessed last week and the week before that and asked you to make moral decisions instead of issuing injunctions. It meant that you had to take some responsibility for your spiritual life, not just during the annual three-day retreat but every day of the year.

In the middle of my junior year, I chose Father McCallin as my confessor because, after living under his supervision for two and a half years, I knew him better than any other priest at the college and thought him the most intelligent man— remember his view of women—I had ever known. He never told me that if I slept with K. I would have to marry her. That didn't follow in strict moral theology, but for me it might as well have been graven in stone, and by this time he knew me pretty well.

So I would confess whatever obvious sins I had indulged in, without getting into the general issues, and he would ask questions that I could anticipate—as I have said, he employed the Socratic method brilliantly—and to which I already had textbook answers and no alternatives. Any other priest would have given the same advice, if more clumsily and less patiently. Perhaps I chose a confessor in order to help me formulate clearly a decision I had already made.

I was not the only Rockhurst man in this position. One man a year ahead of me, a big man on campus, had dated one of K.'s contemporaries who—as we put it in those days—could fall forward without bumping her nose. Faced with the same conflict between morals and desire, he decided to avoid temptation and stopped dating her. Unfortunately for his peace of mind, they sang in a mixed chorus, which meant that she had frequent occasion to take deep breaths. She had also borrowed one of K.'s sweaters, several sizes too small, which she would tug downward. I think he kept his resolve, but not his composure.

One of Father McCallin's other spiritual advisees admitted to having trouble on both counts. He was a man who seemed to attract sins and near occasions of sin—which, at the end of a formal confession, we were supposed to promise to avoid. Father Mac had told him to come to him whenever he needed to make a good confession or just for spiritual advice. As he told the story, he went so often one weekend that Father Mac finally gave up and took him out for a drink, as much for his own nerves as to keep an eye on his penitent.

I wasn't that attractive, and except for K., I didn't have all that many temptations. I dated other girls from CST and some nurses, including the very nice one from my freshman year, but I didn't find them very interesting or desirable. I had one date with an airline stewardess who seemed intimidatingly older and boring at the same time. I saw girls in costume at the Kansas City Art Institute Beaux Arts Ball and knew that they were far out of my league.

Now, with more experience, I realize that I was going through a process of grieving, like the aftermath of a divorce but less definite. If I had not graduated, the separations and reunions might have gone on interminably. But I did. K. had another year of college, and, like Gregory Peck in *The Snows of Kilimanjaro*, I got out of town.

Almus Pater

Does training by men *and* with men *mean more to you? Rockhurst is a college for men. Many of the oldest and best colleges of the United States admit only men, have male faculties, and have developed in both classroom and extracurricular activities a masculine atmosphere.*
—*Rockhurst College brochure*

Today this language may seem more ludicrous than sexist, but in 1951, to someone who had been taught by nuns for eleven years, it could sound attractive. The nuns were in the business of training rather than educating.

The education we got was limited not because the nuns were nuns or because they were women but because they had been given a particular mission in a particular culture. They drilled, or pounded, grammar, arithmetic, catechism, and a great deal of secondary lore and mythology about saints and pious practices into the skulls—Celtic, Teutonic, Italian, whatever kinds bowed before them—of the students in their charge.

And it stuck. For example, just the other day a friend reading a book about Romans and barbarians mentioned Saint Ambrose. Oh, yes, I said, he taught Saint Augustine. Right, said my friend; and he was *very* close to his mother. Saint Monica, I said. If asked, which I wasn't, I could have gone into much greater detail about lives of the saints, drawing on fifteen years of Catholic education.

The nuns didn't just teach; they preached, cajoled, and threatened in order to keep the girls from getting pregnant and the boys from drifting out of the church. The process of training means curbing some natural instincts and redirecting others. Tigers jump? Fine: put a hoop in front of them. Tigers eat meat? Not so good: persuade them to be more selective.

All primary and some secondary education probably has to operate on these premises if the students are to learn the ground rules of the various disciplines. But many Americans, especially Catholics and not excluding most of the nuns, assumed that the women who enforced these necessary limitations were themselves incapable of any larger vision. In practice, the system did give some of us the heady feeling that if we sneaked out and learned something interesting, we were outwitting the nuns.

This attitude toward the classroom may account for the fact that it has taken more than twenty thousand words to get around to discussing the academic side of my college career. Some people might think it odd that the Jesuits didn't jump on us right away, but they have little experience with lower division students. Freshman and even sophomore courses were, and to some extent still are, part of the selective process. Students presumably come because they want an education, not, as in high school, because they have to. Those not prepared, academically or emotionally, for college sort themselves out, often with little regard for faculty concern and retention programs. In the early 1950s, Rockhurst was no more callous or academically elitist than other schools, but in retrospect it is clear that real education took place in upper division courses.

The men who taught at Rockhurst were not inherently smarter or better than the women who had taught me in high school, but they had more and better education, broader outlooks, and a different mission than the nuns at Boonville Catholic High School. Moreover, I was impressed by the fact that most of the Rockhurst faculty called me Mr. Davis, however ironically, rather than Robert. And, except in pickup basketball games, no Jesuit ever hit me upside the head.

In fact, the nuns and the fathers had the same general goal: to prepare us to save our souls. Saint Ignatius Loyola, founder of the Jesuits, was quite explicit about this in *The Constitutions of the Society of Jesus*: "The end of the Society and of its studies is to aid our fellowmen to the knowledge and love of God and to the salvation of their souls." This is the premise on which he based the Jesuit university curriculum.

However, the Jesuits were, true to the stereotype, more subtle about delivering the message. (So subtle, in fact, that I didn't discover the *Constitutions* until 1993. But they hadn't been translated into English until fifteen years after I left Rockhurst.) In my parish school, daily mass was so well understood as part of the routine that it didn't have to be required, and time for weekly confessions was scheduled into the school week.

Saint Ignatius believed "that those who come to the universities of the Society to obtain knowledge should acquire along with it good and Christian moral habits" and that ideally students would hear daily mass, make monthly confessions, and hear sermons on feast days. But he was realistic: those who were not "easily constrained . . . should be persuaded gently and not forced to it nor expelled from the schools for not complying, provided that dissoluteness or scandal to others is not observed in them."

Therefore, the college required attendance at a weekly mass on Fridays and a yearly retreat (see *A Portrait of the Artist as a Young Man* for the scarier and more memorable parts of that ritual and a review in the student paper my freshman year, which praised Father Diebold's deft handling of "the birth, life, and the passion and death of Christ"). Otherwise, Rockhurst paid no formal attention to our practice of the faith. It was assumed—by most of the students as well as the Jesuits—that we would attend mass on Sundays, and it was a positive pleasure to hear it in the college chapel with a few peers rather than crowd into the parish church across the street. For one thing, mass in the chapel took less time: no sermon or long lines at the Communion rail. For another, it seemed less social and more religious. Some of us took things more solemnly: editorials called for spontaneous visits to the chapel, recommended religious vocations, and otherwise outdid the Jesuits in public zeal. I once questioned in print the practice of dedicating formal dances to Our Lady on the grounds that most people paid no attention to the prayer, but, out of piety or prudence, I was careful not to attack the theory behind it.

While the rules did not prescribe practice of the faith, the curriculum emphatically enforced its teaching. The Jesuits didn't tell us pious stories about Saint Augustine; they, or anyway one of them, taught *The City of God*, and a good deal else that was not specifically religious. Saint Ignatius thought that "since the arts or natural sciences dispose the intellectual powers for theology, and are useful for the perfect understanding and use of it, and also by their own nature help towards the same ends, they should be treated with fitting diligence and by learned professors. In all this the honor and glory of God our Lord should be sincerely sought." Four centuries later, the Jesuits held to this end, but, as their recruiting material implied, they did not lean too hard on the means because they were also preparing us to live and work in the secular world.

In fact, so had the nuns. But in college, the stakes were higher and the game more complicated. Take mathematics, which I did reluctantly. Sister Lorena, the principal of my high school, was also its best teacher. She called me Robert, but on the other hand, she never hit me. She taught, with exceptional enthusiasm and good humor for a nun, an overload class in second-year algebra for three students: Jerry Lammers, who went on to get an M.S. in mechanical engineering; Don Vollmer, who got a B.S. in electrical engineering; and me. I must have worked hard at solving the problems because my transcript reveals that I got a 94, only three points below the highest grade I ever got. But I never made any connection between the problems and the general principles or applications implied in them, and Sister Lorena probably and I certainly never realized that I wasn't doing so.

Father Doyle was far from being the worst teacher I had at Rockhurst, and my grades in math weren't any worse than the ones I got in Catholic Marriage or Spanish I. But those I got because I was lazy or inattentive and because the professors were harder to fake out than the nuns or didn't go for the same moves. Father Doyle was not just a math teacher, he was a mathematician, and his lively progress across the blackboard showed me that I had no ear for math the way that some people have no ear for music. I managed to hum enough bars in the key of C and fulfill the requirements—I spent a week in calculus and couldn't even recognize the tune—and was grateful that it wasn't any worse. I bore no animosity toward Father Doyle, who was a very nice man and didn't seem to take my ignorance as a personal affront. I enjoyed his energy and cheerfulness. And later, some of my friends, though not my best friends, were math majors.

Math, like about half of the courses I took, was required. The curriculum and requirements were almost laughably primitive by today's standards, when advising has become more complicated than ordering from an untranslated Chinese menu. The clearest requirement was four years of Latin for a B.A. degree (only three men in my graduating class managed that). Everyone else, including English majors, received a B.S. Father McCallin quoted a former president of Harvard: a B.S. doesn't guarantee that a boy knows any science, but it does guarantee that he doesn't know any Latin.

Everyone was required to take at least four religion courses—Catholic Teaching and Life, Catholic Marriage, Revelation and the Modern Mind, and Bases of Social Reconstruction (drawing heavily on principles from the social encyclicals of the late nineteenth and early twentieth centuries, which responded to socialist and communist theory). These were supposed to ground us in the principles underlying our faith and had the added advantage of deterring students from transferring because no other school would accept the credits. Other religion courses may have been offered, but I never knew anybody who admitted to taking one.

Some otherwise respectable people did major in philosophy, and everyone had to have a philosophy minor as well as what we thought of as a real one: the Art of Thinking (Aristotelian logic, or fun with syllogisms), the Philosophy of Reality (Thomistic metaphysics), the Philosophy of Man, Ethical Principles (what you ought to do), and Applied Ethics (how to apply the principle of double effect to evade inconvenient principles). All were taught from textbooks rather than from the original sources, and Logic was the only course that could be distinguished from religion courses because, as in math, it mattered how you got to the textbook answer. In the other philosophy courses, you knew where you were supposed to end up and could reason backward from that.

Except for the two-semester survey of economics, which must have been mandatory or I wouldn't have taken it, the other requirements looked like those anywhere in the period and were not all that different from current ones: freshman composition, history (European) surveys, math, two semesters of lab science (in my case, biology, the last refuge of the mathless), two years of a foreign language.

Outside of religion and philosophy courses, the professors did not emphasize and in fact rarely mentioned matters of faith, morals, and doctrine; matter and manner of instruction differed little from comparable courses at a secular school. The only specifically Catholic course outside religion and philosophy was in the works of John Henry Cardinal Newman, and that was not required. Probably there was tacit observation of Ignatius's dictum against teaching immoral works, but doubtful ones crept in, and I saw no evidence that the college followed his injunction that "even though a work may be good it should not be lectured on when the author is bad, lest attachment to him be acquired." But the curriculum did make enthusiastic use of his permission to the society to seize on the good parts of pagan authors "like the spoils of Egypt." Normally they didn't go as far as the drama professor who selected an anthology that, he claimed in mock horror to discover, included plays by Jean-Paul Sartre—listed on the Index of Prohibited Books.

No Jesuit would have made that mistake. All of the philosophy and religion courses were taught by Jesuits, of course. Years later, as a faculty member at a Jesuit school, I heard the theory that if a Jesuit was slow to catch on, he was assigned to teach philosophy. If he was too slow for that, he was assigned to teach religion. If he was hopeless even there, he was made an administrator. This didn't seem true at Rockhurst. I couldn't imagine anyone telling Father Gough, our dean, to do anything. His many imitators tried to talk with teeth clenched, and the most popular tag-line, taken from the bulletin board, was, "The following will see Father Gough eee-*med*-iately." I was never important enough to make that list; Father Cahill, the assistant dean, dealt with me. Even after a brief term as an assistant dean myself, I still don't like to go to a dean's office.

The philosophy and religion teachers had an uphill battle against student indifference or active resentment at the requirements. But even these professors were sometimes more interested in *why* than in *what*. And in other courses, a plausible and ingenious answer was, to my relief, perfectly acceptable. They wanted to expand, not channel, the students' minds, and that was refreshing. They were much harder to bullshit than the nuns had been, and that was both refreshing and challenging. And the term and even the concept of "retention rates," sacred to contemporary administrators, had not been invented.

I can remember all of their names and something about their individual styles—better, I imagine, than some recent university graduates can do—partly because, according to sometimes exasperated friends, I remember every damned thing but mostly because Rockhurst was a very small college with a tightly organized curriculum and a small faculty. In four years I had at most seventeen teachers. Almost 60 percent of those were Jesuits, and I'll give odds that no graduate of the twenty-seven Jesuit colleges and universities in the last twenty, perhaps thirty, years can say that. (Between 1962 and 1965, I taught in another branch of the chain, and we had at most two or three Jesuits in a large department. In 1989, I interviewed for a job at still another Jesuit university and talked to faculty and administrators for two days solid without ever seeing a Jesuit.) I think that most of them worked hard at their jobs and cared about what they taught and about the students. Of course, some were more dynamic or had more talent for dealing with young men than did others.

Almus Pater

Although the Jesuits all dressed in cassocks, which looked like floor-length dresses tied rather inefficiently with sashes, they did not as teachers seem noticeably different from the lay professors. For example, Harry Kies taught the survey of European history in dry, understated fashion and seemed to enjoy a book report I constructed without resorting to the tedious straw of fact, and he gave me B's for style, not substance. Father Robert Imbs taught the survey of American history with more outward enthusiasm—he also taught speech and coached the debate team—and presorted sheep from goats by giving three levels of examinations: objective questions to students who could get no better than a C, a mixture of objective and essay questions to students who could get no better than a B, and pure essay questions to students who aspired to A's. (That was his first semester, when he underestimated our stamina. He had to stay more than an hour past the end of the examination period and then read the interminable results. But he learned fast. The final A exam question for the second semester read simply: "Trace the economic, social, and political development of the United States from 1865 to the present, using the outline method.")

In my English major, I took thirteen courses, at least nine of them—ten, if I'm right about the second half of the English literature survey—from two men, Father Robert O'Sullivan, S.J., whom we always called Father O'Sullivan, and Mr. Robert Knickerbocker, whom we referred to, though not to his face, as Knick. (I still have to make an effort to call him Bob.)

I had only three other English teachers. A layman, known as Ducker because he had been a boxer, was very good, but he soon departed for St. Louis University. (In the early 1980s, when my beard was already graying, I encountered him at the Educational Testing Service reading advanced placement essays and reminded him that he had taught me sophomore survey.

He did not seem grateful for the reminiscence, a response I understand better every year.) A Jesuit was sent from Creighton University one year and tried to teach me Shakespeare. I learned more than he thought I did, but he resented the attention I gave to the student newspaper. He did not seem an amiable man.

The third teacher was a recent Rockhurst graduate who directed plays, taught drama courses, and in my senior year offered an English course in contemporary drama. We read and wrote single-spaced one-page reports on three plays a week, and since there were only three students in the class, I was better and more consistently prepared than usual.

I learned something from all three men, but unlike Father O'Sullivan and Mr. Knickerbocker, they were not crucial to my education. I encountered Father O'Sullivan first because he taught what would now be called the honors section of first-year Reading, Writing, and Speaking, to which I was assigned. He stood about six foot six inches and was the most consistently cheerful man on the faculty, and he went out of his way to encourage students. In my case he went too far. Perhaps he knew that I came from a small school and thought that I might feel intimidated by the other students in the class, at least two of whom later went to Johns Hopkins University on graduate fellowships. At any rate, one day not far into the semester he handed back my paper and said, "If you keep this up, I'm going to have to give you an A." Naturally, I stopped doing any work at all. As a teacher, I have never succeeded in emulating his successful methods, but I have not made that one mistake.

Father O'Sullivan also taught the course in Practical Criticism, for which the text was Brooks and Warren's *Understanding Poetry*. As to many of my contemporaries, that book was a revelation: reading was not mere passive skimming to remember characters and plot details but an active encounter that called for as much wit and memory and ingenuity as the reader could muster, and, judging from the analyses in the textbook, a lot more than any of us had. I remember trying to use their analytic techniques on Robert Frost's "Out, Out" and being more pleased with myself than I should have been. But it was the first academic writing assignment that really interested me.

Father O'Sullivan was particularly enthusiastic about writing contests, and he went to great lengths, even typing manuscripts, to encourage his students to enter them. In his upper division courses, he allowed students to substitute a contest entry for a traditional term paper. My first attempt was a review of Margaret Culkin Banning's *Fallen Away* (a Catholic woman divorces a worthless husband, marries a good pagan outside the church, suffers agonies of conscience, and is let off the hook when the ex-husband dies offstage). My enthusiasm for the book, never strong, waned considerably when Father Mac looked at it and said, "Ah, yes, the Catholic Faith Baldwin." A year later I did get an A in Milton, at least in part for writing a book review of Evelyn Waugh's *The Loved One* that won the Catholic Community Library annual book review contest. Even at the time I thought this took the principle of style over substance to ridiculous lengths, though I was grateful for the A. (The substitution turned out to be useful in my scholarly career, but since that was the only course in Milton I ever took, it could have been disastrous for my Ph.D. general examination in Renaissance literature. Fortunately the examiner set, as the only Milton question, a discussion of light and dark imagery in *Paradise Lost*. Even I had heard of that.)

Father O'Sullivan seemed to take a Platonic view of my performances: appearances were mere deceptions cloaking the shining higher plane. Knick regarded me in more skeptical fashion, partly because he was a New Englander and partly because my papers for him—all research papers, subject to the severe limitations of area libraries—never seemed to have much spark. I saved none of them and the only topic I can remember still makes me wince.

However, as moderator of the *Hawk*, the college newspaper, Knick was one of the few teachers who had to curb my active impulses rather than try to prod them, because I devoted far more energy to unofficial than to academic pursuits. But he never seemed to resent the clumsy attempts to subvert the college policies or image, and we didn't resent his cautionary advice. We just realized that we were going to have to be more devious.

I think he knew me pretty well. When the results of the book review contest were announced, he said, "When I heard what you'd chosen, I knew you would win." The more I learned about Evelyn Waugh, who used wit as weapon and shield, the less flattering I found that remark.

We knew more about Knick than we did most of our other teachers: that he had gone to Providence College and Brown University and that he was working on a Ph.D. at the University of Kansas, forty miles west of Kansas City. We knew that his baptismal names were Maximilian Robert and how old he was because one day, when a student said that someone his age couldn't be expected to understand a particular point, Knick drew himself up and said sternly, "I do *not* consider thirty-two to be an advanced age." We knew that if you asked him to do something, he would make a note and spike it. Later we came to believe that when the spike got full, he would strip it into the wastebasket without reading the notes. Then he would repeat the process. The third time we asked him, he would do it immediately on the theory that if it hadn't gone away by that time, it must be significant. I was pleased to learn that a grownup could procrastinate even more efficiently than I could. It was even more important that he was a layman because, though

I did not regard him as what is now called a role model, I could see that he had a life outside the classroom which I had some chance of comprehending.

As a teacher, he had experience with my lethargic phase and once, when I fell asleep in his nineteenth-century English poetry class, asked the other students to get up quietly and leave me. But I heard his request and exited with my classmates. (I should add that I fell asleep far more than once in his and other classes, but he was the only professor who tried to leave me. Father Daues was more charitable: he caught me as I was about to topple onto the concrete floor while asleep in his metaphysics class.)

Like Father O'Sullivan, Knick wanted his students to think about the world outside Rockhurst. He encouraged me to apply for a teaching assistantship in the M.A. program at the University of Kansas when I had never considered graduate work and didn't know what an assistantship was. I don't know what he said in his letter of recommendation—probably something about promise rather than performance—but I did get in, obviously well down the preference list.

(Years later, when as director of the Oklahoma graduate program, I called him to ask about prospective students, he listed the best students who had already taken fellowships. Then, after a pause, he said, "Of course, there's X. He's a late bloomer. But *you* ought to understand that." A few years after that I sent him a postcard from Paris: "Thirty years ago you assigned James Fenimore Cooper's *The Prairie*. I finally got around to reading it in order to give a lecture at the University of Paris. When it's a condition of another trip to Paris, I'll read another Cooper novel." Five years after that, waiting at the Kansas City airport, I called him. Oh, yes, he had received the postcard and had been amused but not surprised at my confession.)

Knick was a layman; and it was hard to think of Father O'Sullivan as a Jesuit because he didn't seem to have the guile or the edge traditionally associated with Jesuits. This could not be said of the two priests from whom I had four courses each, one set from necessity, one from choice.

Father Joseph Freeman, S.J., was my teacher in both freshman religion courses and in both senior philosophy courses. If he had been born thirty years later, he could have been a star of call-in radio or, better still, television, thrusting microphones, awkward questions, and a jaw like a comic-book superhero at flustered guests.

He obviously had more physical energy than his peers. We would see him dressed in a rubber suit chopping wood, and he joined the pick-up basketball games in the field house with enough intensity to shock even a modern NBA official. Retaliation in kind was unthinkable, and some large and rugged undergraduates finally refused to play with him. (A smaller, milder Jesuit joined our games for a while. One evening he was having a particularly frustrating time. I blocked most of his shots and scored over and around him at will. Then, in the post, I passed off and turned to cut for the basket and received a blow full in the jaw. Without thinking, I drove an elbow into his solar plexus. I had showered and dressed before he could get to his feet.)

Father Freeman was the only professor at Rockhurst who did not address his students as "Mr." That took too long. He would pose a question, whirl, point, and shout "Dave!" That meant me. If I did not come up with an immediate and satisfactory answer, the finger would point elsewhere and another abbreviated name would be called. (I think he was prejudiced against people with monosyllabic names like Scott.) It was not safe to sleep in his class, though by my senior year I could wake from a doze and give a plausible answer about an ethical issue because by that time I had heard enough bars of the official line to fake it.

It wasn't possible to fake it in the numerous papers he assigned, but not because he examined them rigorously. We had a theory that he weighed them and gave so many points per pound. Much later I was told that in fact he did page through them, counting and making sure that none of the pages were blank.

If Kansas City Catholics had been given the term "Jesuit" in an association test, most would probably have replied "Freeman." He was the public Jesuit spokesman not because he wanted to be but because he had the best qualifications. He attacked Paul Blanshard's view that American Catholicism was a gigantic conspiracy. He gave a series of public lectures on "God's Law: The Measure of Man's Conduct." He taught Ethics, and on ethical issues he was clear and definite in ways that Good Practical Catholics, serious Protestants, and even news-papermen could understand. He was dynamic in the pulpit. He tried to foster healthy boy-girl relationships.

Perhaps I had already developed an immunity to charisma. At any rate, I can't remember any of his sermons. I do remember one, given at the obligatory Friday college mass, by Father McCallin, who wasn't just prefect of my dormitory and later my confessor but also an intellectual force in the college. He spoke for no more than two minutes about the virtues of the Blessed Virgin. He paused, fixed the congregation with his eye, and said: "And keep your hands off the women." Then he turned abruptly and went back to the altar. Not long, not com-plicated, not, in the usual sense, eloquent, and not of much practical avail. But memorable.

Unlike Father Freeman, he was not much in favor of healthy boy-girl relationships because they distracted the young men from intellectual pursuits. (The word in the Jesuit residence,

Father Gough told me recently, was that if Freeman didn't drive the young men away from marriage, McCallin would drive them into it.) Once at St. Francis Xavier Church across the street a Catholic Youth Organization hayride was announced. "The next thing you know," Father Mac complained, "they'll be saying, 'Fornication will be committed after the eleven o'clock mass'!"

In the four years we lived under the same roof, the only exercise I ever saw Father Mac take was walking back and forth to class. He was as close to being a counterculture figure as the Rockhurst Jesuit community came. For one thing, he lived not with the other Jesuits but with boarding students and a dog, Tray (as in the song, "Old dog Tray, ever faithful, grief cannot drive him away. He is gentle, he is kind, you will never, never find, a better friend than old dog Tray"), and a tomcat whose name I can't remember who, returning battered from a night on the town, was ruefully compared to the young men under his master's charge. For another, Father Mac was recognizable at any distance because he invariably wore a biretta (a brimless cap with three vertical flanges that was so old-fashioned that it seemed revolutionary) and, except on the very warmest days, a cape. I had never seen a cape except in superhero comic books and Erroll Flynn movies. He spoke very precisely and with a full range of vocabulary and would correct our grammar and usage on the theory that "either the young men will speak as I do, or I will begin to speak as they do." And while most professors addressed me as Mr. Davis, in the barracks Father Mac called me "young Davis." God knows that was accurate.

Father Mac's isolation and appearance were by no means the oddest things about him. Among dedicated or anyway indoctrinated Thomists, he professed to be an Augustinian. Saint Augustine's darker and more poetic view of human nature before God seemed much more attractive than Saint Thomas's formulaic treatment of propositions (I am judging strictly on external form, being innocent of the content), and Father McCallin's line of reasoning seemed more subtle and less canned for rebroadcast than the pronouncements in the required religion and philosophy classes. I couldn't wake from a doze and answer one of his questions in his Intellectual History classes because I couldn't predict where he was going even if I knew where he had been. Once a student quoted the official line from Ethics class about a "morally acceptable reason," and Father Mac looked over his spectacles and said, in his rather rasping voice, "Beware of the man with a morally acceptable reason." The implication, of course, was that one could always be manufactured for the occasion; the deeper implication, which he did not pursue, is that morally acceptable reasons have nothing to do with virtue. And because he never talked about virtue—at least in the current moral climate of abstinence—we began to value it.

Like Grandpa Murray, he liked to shock people. Leading an English Club discussion on "the aspects of Christian culture," he argued that "a truth may be both absolute and relative at the same time" and denied the existence of Christian culture as such. This threw the meeting into a confusion which was resolved only when Father O'Sullivan "suggested that the dictionary should be used to define controversial terms." That, as I discovered when I tried it in a paper, did not suit Father Mac's style at all.

Father Mac wasn't the only Ph.D. on the Rockhurst faculty, but he was the only one I encountered on a regular basis. He was an enormously energetic teacher, putting out reams of outlines and other supplementary materials for his courses. He did not believe in memorizing dates—one could always look those up—and his reading lists were wildly eclectic for the time: Tacitus, Ruth Benedict's *Patterns of Culture*, Corneille and Racine,

Piers Plowman, Veblen's *The Theory of the Leisure Class*, Tawney's *Religion and the Rise of Capitalism*, and Orwell's *Nineteen Eighty-Four*—all in one course. In the middle of the term, he would suddenly veer in new directions, bringing in the theories of Pitirim Sorokin, which we had to apply to all of these books, or, in one memorable but abortive attempt at interdisciplinary thought, those of a Rockhurst professor of physics, who alternated with Father Mac in covering the blackboard with symbols in an attempt to find some underlying formula of culture. Even if we didn't read all of the material or follow all of the arguments, which I certainly didn't, we got to watch intellectual gymnastics of a very high order and began to learn some of the moves.

Father Mac was the best Socratic method teacher I have encountered in forty years of higher education. He prodded, teased, questioned. No answer was intelligent enough to pass unquestioned or stupid enough to be dismissed without further examination. If Father Freeman was the public's idea of Jesuit eloquence and forcefulness, Father Mac represented the order's legendary subtlety. This was the McCarthy (Joe, not Gene) era when academics and others were being badgered by Congress and other guardians of political orthodoxy. Father Mac's students kept hoping that he would be called to testify because the senator from Wisconsin would have been discomfited much earlier than he was.

Student writing got even more exacting scrutiny than oral responses. I have kept the papers for his courses, all collaborations with Jim Scott, another bachelor's of science English major who became a professor of English. The comments, however critical, are the only parts I can now read without wincing. He blocked bad metaphors and split infinitives, reproved slang as "expressive but crude." He did not anticipate the move to foster groundless self-esteem: beside an A he complained, "To give this grade is very painful, and the pain lies in seeing the sloppiness of form and sometimes of expression in a piece of work which is carefully thought out and obviously of some ambition."

Because the faculty was small, history majors and minors had to take a course from Father Mac every semester whether we wanted to or not, and most of us wanted to. And because the classes were relatively small and the rosters stable, he got to know our habits of mind and characteristic weaknesses. His comments on our collaborative efforts grew longer and more detailed. On the last of these his comment began, "This paper shows that you are growing, and that is much, and the best, to say of young men." But—and with Father Mac there was always a but—if "in the wide sweep of thinking" we were able, we had neglected to make "the small, definite, detailed connections, with the evidence, well-thought out, of their relationships," and our style in general left much to be desired, including the "outstanding gaucheries" that he marked. But we were used to the sting, and his conclusion made us forget it: "The idea you have in the paper is well worth a book, and would make a splendid doctor's dissertation."

Since I had not even been admitted to an M.A. program, writing a book or dissertation seemed wildly beyond my ambition or ability to conceive. Like all great teachers, Father Mac had a clear sense that he was part of a process, and he knew how to point his students to the next stage. For the most part, he did this by concentrating on the sweep of the intellect across centuries and ideologies, never subduing his style but never mistaking it for content. Sometimes, though, as in his sermon on chastity, he would deliver oracular pronouncements. The one I remember best is "Spend your life before you are thirty preparing for what you will do after you are thirty." I actually followed this advice, though I might have anticipated the date if my career in graduate school had been more coherent.

Aside from these dicta, I don't remember much of what my teachers said about any particular book or idea or even of the way they said it. But it was important that they did say it, because like my first-generation peers in college, I had never heard it said before, in that way. My family had plenty of intelligent people, but even that self-confident bunch would not have described themselves as scholars. My father was shrewd and could display depths of awareness and even of knowledge that he mostly kept hidden. My mother read widely and could keep a discussion going for long and interesting periods. Her father, Grandpa Murray, would with the right kind of training and attitude have made a good Jesuit.

But like many provincial people—and I don't just mean geographically—they were broadly skeptical rather than critical, and though they could be interesting, they were not disinterested. That is, they did not pursue a line of inquiry for its own sake, and they seemed more concerned with what they were going to say next than in examining someone else's premises and method of reasoning. In short, they did not seem to be aware of participating in a dialogue with people oceans and centuries removed.

And so the men who spoke at my orientation were right: liberal education provided us not with substance or practical skills but with an attitude toward language and thought, space and time that took me a lot farther from Boonville than I expected.

The author's boyhood home. (Photo by Bert McClary.)

Parade on Main Street, Boonville, Missouri.

The author, left, and two other freshmen being collegiate outside the barracks.

The author, extreme left, at a dance during his freshman year.

Students relaxing in a room in the barracks, 1954, just before they were destroyed. (From the *Rock* yearbook, courtesy of Rockhurst College.)

The author, working on his persona, with co-editors Bob Tumino and Jim Friedl, 1953. (From the *Rock* yearbook, courtesy of Rockhurst College.)

By Bob Davis

Logo for the author's column in the *Rockhurst Hawk*. (Courtesy of Rockhurst College.)

The author and Jim Scott at an English Club meeting—probably, to judge from the socks, about 1954.

The author, seated right, at an editorial committee meeting of the *Hawk*.

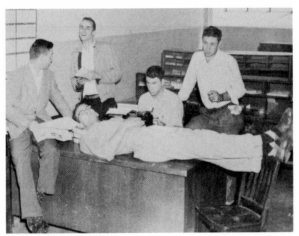

The author, recumbent, at the end of his career as a college journalist. Jim Scott, seated at the typewriter, and Bob Wurtz, standing, right, also became college professors. (From the 1955 *Rock* yearbook, courtesy of Rockhurst College.)

Joseph A. McCallin, S.J., advisor and confessor. (From the 1955 *Rock* yearbook, courtesy of Rockhurst College.)

M. Robert Knickerbocker, Jr., moderator of the newspaper and professor of English. (From the 1955 *Rock* yearbook, courtesy of Rockhurst College.)

The author's senior picture, 1955. (From the *Rock* yearbook, courtesy of Rockhurst College.)

Dr. Meulemans, biology professor, with the author and his parents at graduation. (From the 1955 *Rock* yearbook, courtesy of Rockhurst College.)

The author, center, unaccountably cheerful, flanked by the editor and senior reporter at the Great Bend, Kansas, *Daily Tribune*, summer, 1955.

Manly Exchanges

In a college for men, opportunities are at hand for a manly exchange of ideas and the generous "give-and-take" which prepares you to deal with people in later life.

—Rockhurst College brochure

Of all the recruiting brochure promises, this comes closest to the original language and intention of the *Constitutions*, which encouraged masters to have students of "humane letters" practice by "composing in a good style and delivering well what they have composed" and having "those studying the higher branches, engage in disputations often." By 1951, the Jesuits had to abandon Ignatius's desire that the students speak Latin as a matter of course, and we never had a chance to hear our professors "hold disputations with one another, always preserving the proper modesty and having someone preside to stop the debate and give the doctrinal solution."

Liberal arts students held almost as an article of faith that we learned more in bull sessions in the dorms, cafeteria, and lounge than we did in class. Sometimes this was fairly obvious bad faith, on a parallel with the fear of nuclear holocaust that we claimed drove us to seek consolation at Leo's Blatz Tavern.

The people eager to go to Leo's—mostly the people a year ahead of me in the barracks—would have insisted that they were manly, but they were not notable for exchanging ideas. It took a while, even in a small liberal arts school, to find people who had ideas and were also willing to give me a turn to talk.

In practical terms, this meant that I had to break into the circle of the raging urbanites from Kansas City. The usual way of assimilating, joining a fraternity, didn't really arise. Rockhurst did have two fraternities, Alpha Delta Gamma (ADG), a social fraternity, and Alpha Phi Omega (APO), a service fraternity composed, as I recall, of former boy scouts.

Since the ADGs didn't have a house, and since the barracks boys were a tightly knit group with whom you could get as drunk and noisy as you liked without having to worry about group social probation, rituals, or additional fees, none of us saw the point of the social fraternity. In subsequent years I did not avoid the company of men who belonged to it, but I never sought them out, partly because their values seemed antithetical to those I was learning from the teachers I respected but mostly because of an inherent dislike of organizations.

I don't think that any of the resident students belonged to APO either, but I could applaud and even share its values as long as I didn't have to practice them. Some of its members I came to know and like. It was useful to have friends in this organization because its members took attendance at Friday mass, and some of them would fiddle the record if given notice that you intended to cut. I don't remember asking anyone to do this, but as an upperclassman I was invited to some of the fraternity's beer and poker parties. This was mutually advantageous. They were not allowed to have beer at official gatherings, and since I was a well-known nonjoiner, my very presence was enough to make the party unofficial. Our classes in ethics had taught us well. I benefited because the APO members, trustworthy and clean as well as helpful, were far less competent poker players than my high school friends.

There was also a Jesuit honor fraternity, Alpha Sigma Nu, composed largely of seniors, but no one from the barracks or Hanley House was invited to join that—not because we were second-class citizens but because each of us, lacking "the salutary and refining influence of his parents and of his home," was grade-point-average challenged, to use a modern euphemism. I don't recall that any of us suffered agonies because of our exclusion.

But as a freshman I was barely aware of these organizations and not noticeable enough to be recruited even as a counter-member. My first real contacts with the natives came in my classes. I had been placed in the "high" sections of religion, English, and perhaps history, where I was the only resident student. This wasn't especially daunting. Up to this point, I had taken it for granted that I could read faster and remember more than anyone around me. This was no longer a safe assumption. My new classmates weren't much quicker than I was and perhaps not even more intelligent, but they were a lot better educated, and their verbal and intellectual sophistication went well beyond anything I had encountered.

This realization could have had one of two effects: made me work ferociously hard to catch up or put me into a depression. In fact, I stroked along in my classes, doing a little more work than I had in high school, appreciating my classmates' performance, and making a cocoon for myself in the barracks.

The physical education classes were another matter. The majority of students had never played organized sports, or whatever it was we did at Boonville Catholic, and I discovered that I could compete with all but the best basketball players and with anyone on the softball field. In one game, already a laugher in which I had several hits right-handed, I took up my stance from the other side of the plate. An important native—a class officer, speaker, actor, member of the Sodality of Our Lady—thought that I was being condescending and insisted heatedly that I bat from my normal position. I didn't exactly point like Babe Ruth, but I told him to calm down because I knew what I was doing. It is still gratifying to remember that I ripped a line drive off his leg.

As the joke about training mules by kindness says, first you have to get their attention. Impressing the natives socially and intellectually took longer. However, under the mockery of the St. Louis contingent in the barracks and with some talent for protective mimicry, I had already begun to modify my Little Dixie Missouri drawl, and contact with Kansas Citians helped burr off the rest. And the folly of trying to act too sophisticated too soon had been pointed out to me. I decided that I had arrived when a local sophisticate, famous for his success with women, said that I seemed pretty sharp for someone who wasn't from Kansas City. I took that as a compliment. (Years later, the son of a famous literary critic expressed surprise that I had understood a complicated point very quickly. By that time I had enough confidence to reply, "Just because I talk funny doesn't mean I'm stupid.")

Another way of meeting natives was to engage in extracurricular activities. Intramural athletics didn't count because we tended to stick with the people we came with, so that the Rockhurst High Yankees stuck together and I played basketball for three years with a shifting cast from the barracks. (By our senior year these divisions had blurred to such a degree that the Yankee quarterback was from as far south in Kansas City as you could go and I played with a motley assortment that even included a business major.)

But even in my freshman year the placement in advanced classes and my choice of drama as the sole elective began to take me outside the barracks into new circles. I discovered that coming from a small town and an even smaller school was not entirely a handicap. At my high school, everyone had to do pretty much everything, so it didn't occur to me that I had to specialize in any one activity.

I don't remember why I enrolled in drama the second semester of my freshman year. None of the barracks crowd was even remotely interested in that kind of thing. Father O'Sullivan may have encouraged me, since he had heard me speak lines I had written and may have figured that I could do better with someone else's. I had been in plays in high school, and my assignment at Rockhurst wasn't burdensome: I played the part of a dead man (and learned to play Hearts) in *Our Town*. On the theory that this was not enough work for two hours of credit, the director sent me to the College of St. Teresa to read for the production of Paul Claudel's *The Tidings Brought to Mary*. As I have already said, I got the role of a leprous medieval church architect. I was thin enough to look sickly, and there wasn't much competition, and for weeks I trudged seventeen blocks through the snow to CST for rehearsal.

The production had a number of problems, chief of which was turning the flowery translation of Claudel's French into something that sounded like human speech. The biggest difficulty with blocking was the leprosy-transmitting kiss, which had to look like a kiss but not be a kiss. This seemed a bit cautious, but since the actress was intimidatingly older and not very attractive to me, I didn't raise objections, which wouldn't have been heard anyway. My biggest acting challenge was carrying the lead actress (who weighed at least 130 pounds and wasn't all that happy about having a provincial freshman as romantic lead) up a flight of three stairs and depositing her on a dias. Since I weighed no more than 160, this was always exciting for both of us.

But I never did drop her, I remembered my lines and delivered them not too woodenly, and I got through the play's run without disgracing myself. One night I did loop two very similar speeches and paralyzed the rest of the cast, but I said something poetic sounding and they recovered enough to say something vaguely relevant and the play was poetic drama and didn't make a whole lot of sense anyway and somehow we got back on track. Father Freeman came back stage afterward, jaw out-thrust, to congratulate us on a moving performance.

After that, I figured I'd better not push my luck. Moreover, I had seen a still picture of myself in tights and doublet, and I was already self-conscious enough about my appearance without subjecting myself to more humiliation. And theatrical types didn't, on the whole, seem to be my kind of people. So I gave up acting, as I had given up organized basketball, without a pang.

At the beginning of my sophomore year, having decided that I wasn't going to be a jock or an actor, I decided to use my experience on the *Cooper County Record* and join the college newspaper staff.

This turned out to be useful in a number of ways: the editors tried with some success to break me of some of my worst stylistic mannerisms; the stories I covered helped me learn something about the college and its students; after a while a by-lined column gave me a certain status that sometimes verged on notoriety; writing for the paper brought me more favorable notice from Knick than my classwork ever did; and ultimately my service on the staff led to what honors the college conferred on me.

I discovered something I could do pretty well that gave instant gratification. In that period the World War II veterans had departed, the anarchic nest of McCallinites who ran the paper my freshman year had graduated, and the Depression babies were a small talent pool. I moved rapidly up the masthead, partly because one of my immediate predecessors and superiors fell victim to the draft and the other developed senioritis.

In fact, the staff of my freshman year didn't present a tough act to follow. The resident poet won statewide honors for things like: "Between the thorns, / before the bloom, The silky shining spider spins / his dew-dropped web." When last heard from he was a sales representative, which supports Flaubert's view that inside every clerk is the wreckage of a poet. The humorous columnist concentrated on personalities, student and faculty, and gave ironic advice on how to be a college man.

The editorials called for school spirit, blood donations, Christianity in Christmas, better study habits, religious vocations, and serious issues in college elections. Those included the need for a student lounge, "better disposal facilities" in the cafeteria, crucifixes in all classrooms, abolition of hazing, corsages at formal dances, and the student court. In fact, most of these suggestions were adopted.

By the time I joined the staff, the verse had become less pretentious, though the editorials remained responsible and dull. But the staff wasn't, and for three years the *Hawk* office was like a semisecret clubhouse to which only a select group had entry, a place to relax and play cards between classes, to complain about problems that everyone shared, and to try to think of ways to evade the fairly mild control over what we printed. Not much was needed, even in the columns that didn't serve as a campus bulletin board. We thought—or I did—that the paper should act as a gadfly to stir the college to life. Our campaigns were pretty revolutionary. We came out for decent dress at the mass that opened the college year (and were accused of pharisaism in a letter signed "An humble publican"); against vandalism, hardly noticeable by today's standards, in the student lounge; for attentiveness during the prayers that began every class; for class officers if they were actually given something to do (responded to by student council and class officers in various meetings, resolutions, and apologias); and, most daringly—Knick remembers it better than I do—for a reexamination of the college's practice of using student teaching assistants in laboratory courses.

Fortunately, this priggish self-importance played only a minor role in my work on the *Hawk*, which became the natural center of my campus social and intellectual life. Of course, we did have to put out a newspaper, but it appeared only twice a month—enough to establish a rhythm without being arduous. There was a sense of shared, if not very difficult, craft in writing, rewriting, composing headlines, making up the pages as neatly and harmoniously as possible, gathering for final late-night sessions at the Y Drive-In near the Plaza, and going down to the print shop to put the paper to bed.

Actually, what we did there was watch the slowest apprentice fumble with page makeup. This exasperated me because I had done enough printing to know how incompetent he was. But it was a union shop, and we weren't allowed to touch anything. One day, however, the apprentice dropped a galley and looked helplessly at the slugs scattered over the floor. "Give me that," I said, took the galley, picked up and arranged the type, ran a proof, and reordered the slugs. He stood there dumbly, and the real printers were careful not to notice the scab laying hands on their materials.

Before long, I was given a regular by-lined feature titled "Thoughts from Abroad." It was supposed to reprint news and absurdities culled from other college newspapers, but as soon as I thought I could get away with it, I turned it into a personal column. We still had to be careful about the spacing of the last word in the title.

In my junior year, I became some kind of sub-editor. In my senior year I seemed to have a different title every issue, but in fact I was one of the head honchos, responsible for recruiting new staff members, putting the paper together (in my senior year literally—none of us knew a thing about paste-up, and in self-defense the nonunion shop hired me to moonlight as makeup man), and maintaining a proper atmosphere of decorum in the office and pages of the *Hawk*.

The recruiting brochure had promised that extracurricular activities would give the student "opportunities to develop his particular talents and interests, and to form lasting friendships." This was true of the *Hawk*. The plural did not apply, but as far as I was concerned, and still am, quality far outweighs quantity.

I don't want to embarrass this friend unnecessarily, so I'll call him Jim Scott. During our freshman year, we didn't know each other, and though we may have had some of the same classes, I don't know that we ever spoke to each other. But in the *Hawk* office we were thrown together because it soon became clear that we would at some point take over the paper.

Jim had joined the *Hawk* staff and served under the leadership of some legendary eccentrics while I had been messing about with athletics and drama, so he had a year's seniority, but he never tried to pull rank because he had an open and friendly nature and because I had some professional experience, or whatever my job at the *Cooper County Record* amounted to.

We ran the paper smoothly enough, and it became a minor element in my friendship with Jim. We were both English majors and history minors, and we had complementary qualities that helped us work well together on papers for Father McCallin and keep up a running conversation which has stretched, with long intervals, for forty years.

Jim was not just an intellectual whetstone; he filled the gap in my social life created when my barracks peers decamped. We began to double-date. Until his marriage, Jim had deplorable taste in girlfriends, favoring nurses rather than girls from St. Teresa's, though to be fair it was my date from St. Joseph's who announced that of course blacks and whites had different and incompatible kinds of blood. But he never seemed to get quite as entangled as I did.

In our senior year, we played for the same intramural basketball team and even, one afternoon, for Kansas City University. We wanted to shoot some baskets, but the Rockhurst team was using the field house. Kansas City University, not yet part of the University of Missouri system, had just begun intercollegiate basketball, and one of us said, "Why not go over there and try out?"

It wasn't a long walk, and the coach was grateful for any bodies who showed up. We filled out some paperwork—fraudulently—and trotted onto the court. Some of the more talented athletes were still playing intramural football, so the squad was even more motley than usual. The scrimmage was strictly run and gun, and I was having a really good day, stealing passes, hitting jump shots, playing tight defense. The coach was delighted.

Then we noticed on the sidelines a Rockhurst graduate who had entered the KCU law school. He kept staring at us, and the coach must have wondered why we were staying near the opposite sideline. Finally we realized that enough was enough, and at the end of the scrimmage we told the coach that we didn't think we could help the team and wouldn't be back. He seemed very disappointed and tried to talk us out of it, but we remained humbly adamant.

Looking back, it seems unlikely that Jim and I became and would remain friends. We were both active—years later, when I interviewed for a job in Jim's department, his colleagues found it difficult to believe that all that energy could be contained in one room—and we shared a sense of mischief. But I have been five minutes early on every occasion in my life, while at that time one could not predict how late Jim would be. I always knew the shortest distance between two points; Jim had at that time almost no idea of where he was in his own home town, and when I talked to him recently said that he liked to *be* places but hated to drive to them. Jim was (and is) expansive, open, and catholic in his choice of friends; I was in my pseudo-Byronic phase, trying to be sardonic and exclusive, as censorious of his taste in unsuitable friends as an exsmoker in a room full of addicts. He was president of the senior class; I was apolitical at my most engaged. He was an honors student; I, to put it mildly, was not. Faculty members (not Knick or Father Mac) who regarded him as promising material pressed Significant Catholic Writers on him, and he took a course in Newman. I, regarded as frivolous and left to my own devices, took modern drama and narrowly escaped contamination by Sartre. In a contest based on Evelyn Waugh's biography of the Jesuit martyr Edmund Campion, he placed ahead of me; I placed higher in writing about *The Loved One*. I was quick; he was steady. As it turned out, I became a bibliographer and student of the transmission of texts; he travels the world making videos.

One of the few things Rockhurst men didn't talk about was friendship, so I don't have a canned definition from those days. Today I'd say that it rests on the ability to share and continue a discourse with someone who can keep up.

Jim was my only close friend, but a number of my contemporaries could pace and for that matter outrun me. I began to associate with the day-hops partly because the original barracks group had dispersed, partly because the classes were becoming more interesting and gave us something to talk about, and partly because we had begun to sort ourselves into majors and to develop the sense of elitism that our more challenging teachers were careful to foster.

This attitude may have begun to leak to the outside world, and in Father Gough's recruiting letter of March 1954, he was careful to deny the implied charge that "all our boys are geniuses or bookworms. They are red-blooded Americans. Many are just average Joes scholastically." Like many pronouncements from above in the 1950s, these were not protested but simply ignored, and the editorial pages of the last issues of the *Hawk* my senior year were dominated by assertions of or attacks on intellectual elitism.

One unsigned feature attacked "Cinemascope Collegians" who acted as though they were on a movie set, regarded college as a right, and forgot about the corresponding duties. An editorial titled "A Select Set" and signed M. K. attacked "The sedulous sectarians of pseudo-intellectualism" who "fashion profound, obtruse [sic] questions—questions delightfully complex and confused, meaning nothing but being actually very time-consuming," "attend the various campus 'intellectual' gatherings and energetically criticize the whole discussion," and "appear strained and burdened as if handling some ponderous problem."

The two pieces were separated by the regular columnist's comments on "Snobs and Slobs," or students of the liberal arts and the business majors who slightly outnumbered us in the graduating class. The column began with caricature but tried to go further. I quote at length not just because I wrote it but because it is a small part of the larger Eisenhower-era concern about the individual and corporate society initiated by David Riesman's distinction between inner versus outer direction in

The Lonely Crowd (1950) and continued in, among many other books and articles, William Whyte's *The Organization Man* (1956). And also because it shows that, at twenty, I had some understanding of the social issues implied in my being in college at all.

> The business majors are all red-blooded American boys [perhaps I had seen Father Gough's brochure], convinced that America is the greatest thing since the invention of alcohol and that people who spend their time reading poetry and indulging in conversations about philosophy, history, literature, and the more abstruse aspects of mathematics are a little less than masculine, susceptible to liberal ideas, and slightly punch drunk.

The snobs, I conceded, "display a lack of respect for hallowed American insituations [sic again; our proofreading was somewhat impressionistic] and, to a lesser degree, of money *qua* money. In other words, many of them are just not normal." With less irony, or whatever it was, I acknowledged,

> It was very well to pursue knowledge for its own sake in former times, when the sons of the aristocracy or the moneyed class indulged in the arts and letters because it was the thing to do, a thing which differentiated them from those less fortunate. A liberal education. . .was a form of conspicuous consumption.

My use of this last phrase doesn't mean that I had actually read Veblen's *Theory of the Leisure Class* in Father McCallin's class, but at least I had picked up the term that was widely recognizable, thus proving M. K.'s case.

I was less tolerant of the business major who, in my characterization,

> is often guilty of a brand of myopic materialism, which is close to slavery to the economy. For Catholic young men, this position is singularly opposed to their religious views. The philosophy of many of them is not, "How may I become a better man?"

which should be the question asked by the arts major, but another question, "What's in it for me?"

Since the question had already been answered in the Rockhurst recruiting brochure, it seems unfair to blame the business majors for materialism. More interesting in retrospect is the degree to which I and some of my classmates had been assimilated into the ethos of elitism. I pointed out that "at least nine-tenths of responsible positions are held by arts majors," but even then I realized that this elite had less power than pretension.

Some of my classmates went a bit too far. A little earlier, a group circulated a petition demanding that all seniors be required to wear coats and ties. This would "improve the stature of the entire college along with the individual's well being, would set the seniors off from the underclassmen and give example for the whole school to follow." Since many of us believed that dressing sloppily was partial compensation for the absence of coed glamor, a counterpetition was sponsored by a man who later became a college president, demanding that socks and jocks be substituted as mandatory apparel. The sartorial elitists retired, grumbling about the great unwashed.

Academically, there was, or seemed to be to those who shared it, a healthier kind of elitism. Rockhurst offered very few gut courses, and most self-respecting students refused to take them. Not that we were indifferent to grades. In the drama course I took with two other students, one—the M. K. of the editorial—said to me, "Bob, you need to work harder." I replied that while this was no doubt true—it usually was—how did that concern him? "Because I figure that either you will get an A, [the future college president] will get a B, and I will get a C, or you will get a B, John will get a C, and I will get a D—and I can't stand a D." One math major did get the only C in music appreciation that anyone had ever heard of. I would like to think that this disproves the theory that math and musical talents are related, but the real reason is simpler. The teacher announced that he was going to play Schubert's *Surprise Symphony*. He lowered the needle. Nothing happened. "Surprise!" said the math major.

The English department offered journalism courses, but I spent three years working for the college newspaper without taking one because Knick convinced me that I wouldn't learn anything. This seemed a compelling reason, so perhaps the system worked. I did take Philosophy of Education in my senior year, but that was because, late one night at Probasco's Drag'n Inn, the professor practically begged me to enroll so that he would have someone to talk to besides jock education majors. I did, mostly because I didn't want to spend a whole semester on Newman.

Most students, or at least the ones worth talking to after class and in the cafeteria, majored in history or English, and everybody minored in philosophy, so the distinction between arts and business majors was blurred. Some of the science majors, whom we knew from the required courses spread over all four years, were well within the pale because they were obviously bright. Some math majors had a sense of humor and other human qualities, but most physics majors were just weird, education majors beneath notice, and business majors not quite beneath contempt, just above the level of the evening school program, where even women were allowed to sneak in under cover of darkness.

In fact, the college made good on the brochure's promise that there would be a manly exchange of ideas. Any day in the cafeteria one could get into a debate on almost any subject. Some people got frustrated and overreached themselves, like the man who accused an opponent of being a "suede-o intellectual" and never lived it down. Others resorted to questionable methods of refutation, like the man who picked up his pie and smushed it in his opponent's face. But mostly we picked each other's arguments to pieces, trying to reduce them to absurdity, going for the jugular.

Some students, mostly history majors, formed under Father McCallin's leadership the Wrangler's Club, where they presented papers for debate. Of the eight original members, three went on to get doctorates; three taught history at the college level; two became attorneys. Their topics were hardly inflammatory, at least from the Jesuit Counter-Reformation viewpoint: "The Intrinsic Immorality and Heinous Character of Competitive Activity, and Particularly as Manifested in the Capitalistic Economy and in Athletics," by a future history professor; "The State, of Its Nature, Breeds Irresponsibility, and, Like Anything that Breeds Irresponsibility, Is Likely to Be Buried in Hell," by a future lawyer; "That [without the capital letters, for some reason] the beatific vision and complete knowledge of God is man's prime end" by a future physicist who now leads a group of charismatic Catholics; "The Decadent Plight of our Society with Regard to the Liquor Traffic and the Repeal of the Eighteenth Amendment"; and "That the Study of Those Branches of Knowledge Referred to as the Natural Sciences Is a Serious Offence Against the Virtue of Prudence and a Perversion of the Intellect." I don't know what happened to the last two speakers.

The last topic seemed reasonable enough to me, but the format was too formal and onerous for my tastes, and the Wranglers seem to have collapsed from their own seriousness. Later Father Mac and a few other professors sponsored more impromptu Sunday morning discussions that operated at a somewhat higher level than our cafeteria arguments.

These encounters taught us that there was a big world out there, full of complicated ideas and very bright people, but they made it seem more interesting than intimidating. We were taught that going for the knockout punch was a mistake made only by the stupid and dogmatic. Instead, work on your timing, watch for an opening, and when your opponent had over-reached himself, counterpunch. Saint Thomas, who answered the questions he asked, was a weaker tactician than Socrates, who asked questions about what other people said. This training was useful in class, in cafeteria sparring, and in what I came to regard as my real life on campus.

The brochure was wrong about one thing: this kind of give and take, argument as blood sport, has not proved to be the best preparation for dealing in later life with people accustomed to genteel forms of discourse. It infuriates or puzzles them. Twenty years after I graduated, a student in one of my honors seminars at the University of Oklahoma complained that I didn't make her feel smart. From the example of my best teachers, I had not realized that this was part of my job.

War:

An Inconvenience

During my college years, the draft was a fact of life, but even while the Korean War was going on, there wasn't any resistance to the draft. Neither was there tremendous upsurge of patriotic fervor to serve in Korea or lust for the experience of battle, as there had been in World War I. The Korean War seemed necessary but not interesting.

Some people had been outraged when, a month before I graduated from high school, President Truman had removed Gen. Douglas MacArthur as commander of forces in Korea after he had threatened to carry the war into China. But most of the indignation came from people well beyond draft age, and most

Americans, on reflection, were quite willing to let MacArthur fade away as he had promised in his address to a joint session of the House and Senate. Joe McCarthy and other Red-hunters still wanted to know who in the state department had lost China, but not even they seriously advocated fighting a war to get it back.

I don't know that my generation thought much about this, though we sometimes reacted when our elders did. None of us particularly wanted to fight in Korea, but a surprising number volunteered for the air force or navy to avoid the army. Others asked their draft boards to call them. Some went because they couldn't think of anything else to do at the time and "active duty" sounded better than just hanging around. The older generation tended to approve because the army was regarded as a cross between reform school and finishing school. When a boy came out, he would be a man.

Most of the people I knew were content with a slower process. None of my high school class went directly into the real service, as we thought of it, though one may have joined the National Guard and one was drafted out of a good engineering job after we graduated from college and sent to White Sands Proving Ground to do highly technical jobs like picking up cigarette butts. Enough people wanted out of Cooper County badly enough to volunteer that the draft board didn't pay much attention to the rest of us.

Our parents worried more than we did. In fact, a few months after I turned eighteen in 1952, Dad split his ticket for the first time in his life to vote for Eisenhower with the rest of the family because Ike promised to go to Korea and end the war. I had not known that Dad valued me that highly.

Rockhurst College, which had pronouncements on almost everything else, had nothing whatever to say about military service. This may have been due to embarrassment. In the late

1940s, the football coach was a member of the reserves, and he persuaded most of the team to join so that they wouldn't be subject to the draft and could pick up a little money on the side. This worked marvelously—until the Korean War erupted in 1950 and a lot of reserves, including the baseball star Ted Williams, were recalled to active duty. That was the end of the Rockhurst football team.

Rockhurst didn't have a ROTC unit, and we didn't miss it. My friends at the University of Missouri had to spend two years in ROTC because it was a land grant university, and they bitched about the meaningless details and general waste of time. Rockhurst left students to their own devices.

Most Rockhurst students came out of the Kansas City Catholic school system, which some years earlier had abolished the eighth grade on principles I never understood or have now forgotten. Most of my classmates were, for the first time in my experience since first grade, my age. At seventeen, we were too young to be drafted. Those who finished a year of college successfully and were "in the prescribed upper portion of the male members of their class" did not have to pass the nation-wide test given to those who wished to apply for the 2-S student deferment. Of course, those who got the 2-S were eligible for the draft until they were thirty-six, but most of us couldn't imagine ever being that old.

Draft boards didn't have to accept the results of the test or the successful completion of a year of college. Most did; some refused to give special treatment to college students. But only a few men in good academic standing were drafted out of Rockhurst. One fought a rear-guard action he was sure to lose, and periodically would sit crooning in drunken anticipation, "I will be drafted and I will be killed." (He was drafted, and at Fort Riley he screamed so convincingly during bayonet drill that he was made a section leader. By the time he got to Korea, fighting had stopped, and he wrote, "Here I am on a hill overlooking Pusan, Korea, surrounded by the ugliest whores in the whole world.")

Some of my Rockhurst classmates enlisted. One even paid for a hernia repair so that he could join the navy. My ex-roommate joined the marines and claimed to have become a sergeant within six months. Another from my original group joined the air force at the end of his sophomore year. Several classmates joined the NAVCAD program and went into flight training at Pensacola. This was regarded as more enterprising than transferring to Central Missouri State College, the traditional alternative for those who wearied of the struggle at Rockhurst.

Most of the time we didn't think about the draft or the war. We might occasionally cite it as a source of incapacitating anxiety when we blew an assignment or cut class to head for a tavern, but we didn't expect anyone to believe it and we said it with a strong dose of self-parody.

The topic was a leit-motif in the college newspaper. An editorial in the first issue of my sophomore year urged students to "Stick With It" ("it" being school), rather than enlist. The reasoning seems quaint even to those who remember the period. First, "the acknowledged primary duty of any Catholic is to persevere in his chosen station of life, using whatever abilities God gave him. For the student, this means that his chief obligation at the moment is to remain a student." Then, beside the practical reasons, is the morally acceptable one:

> The student who values his faith in God, his religious beliefs and his moral integrity has good cause to question the prudence of voluntarily exchanging the atmosphere of a Catholic campus for that of an army training camp. The habits of mind and action cultivated in a Christian scholastic discipline prepare the young

man better than he knows for dealing with the temptations he must inevitably face, once the protection of that discipline is cast aside.

However, most references to the draft sound less like John Kennedy Toole's character, besotted in scholasticism, in *A Confederacy of Dunces* and more like a Max Shulman farce. The draft was a lottery, and you took your chances. Late in 1952 General Lewis B. Hershey, head of the Selective Service System, anounced that a manpower shortage would not become acute until the following June, which, some of us felt, put us in double jeopardy from the draft and from the husband-hunters at CST. A few months later, it seemed possible that fathers might be drafted and, in General Hershey's words, "We certainly must look toward the colleges with something more than an appraising eye." This occasioned my verse:

> Nineteen-year-olds
> Don't be so bold.
> Those winters in Korea
> Are awfully cold.

Fortunately, the Korean armistice was signed in June 1953 (a few months after President Eisenhower gave the French money to combat the uprising in Vietnam and the Viet Minh invaded Laos), making the draft a temporary inconvenience and sometimes a welcome escape from the rigors of college life. As another one of my verses indicates, we could afford a more casual attitude.

JUST A MOAN ON SERVICE

> Waiting for the draft, boys,
> Waiting for the draft.
> Shall I learn a trade, boys?
> Shall I learn a craft?

War

> Should I join the navy, boys,
> Should I break a leg?
> Don't worry, you'll go crazy, boys,
> Let's go tap a keg.
>
> Waiting for the service, boys.
> Waiting for the war.
> Am I still too nervous, boys,
> Should I drink some more?
>
> Sweating out deferments, boys,
> Now's no time to laugh.
> Life has no allurement, boys,
> Waiting for the draft.

The content of this verse will be scarcely comprehensible to people like my son who have grown up in the age of the all-volunteer army. The tone will seem incredibly frivolous to those who demonstrated against the draft during the 1960s. But in 1954, tone and content impressed enough people that it shared (with a poem by a girl from CST) the award for best verse in a college newspaper in Missouri.

Late in 1954 we did have to think about the draft because the government announced that no one who entered the service after January, 1955, would receive benefits under the GI Bill. Some people tried to volunteer for the draft and discovered that the quotas were filled. The only alternative was to enlist, and that required a commitment of three years rather than two. I thought about it briefly, but I did not anticipate needing the benefits and I figured that the new policy meant there wouldn't be much call for my services. Besides, though I'm not sure I put it in those terms, I was afraid that if I broke momentum, I might never regain it. Only one man I knew actually enlisted, and I had always regarded him as an idiot.

I think I still have my draft card, which by law I had to have on my person and in practice was essential for identification at bars once I reached legal age or when the waitress had trouble with subtraction. I may have kept my final classification card. Technically it was possible for me to have escaped the Korean War and whatever it was that followed and to have been drafted any time up to 1970 for the Vietnam war. In fact, by the time I stopped being a student, I was a teacher and then a father. Some of my friends from high school (I didn't stay in touch with many people from college) served in the peacetime army, and though I envied their travels in Europe, I did not regret my civilian status.

Oh, yes, the poem. Years later I discovered that it was based on the poem "Rally Round the Flag." When I wrote it, I thought I was parodying William Empson's parody, "Just a Smack at Auden." So much for Milton's theory that a poet needs to master all knowledge. The Muse takes care of her own.

Invaluable Contacts

Rockhurst's location in a high-employment area affords ample opportunities for part-time work.

Why not make invaluable contacts now by becoming acquainted with business and professional leaders, and with the opportunities offered by business firms and institutions at home?

—Rockhurst College brochures

On a day-to-day basis, the professors and courses I took did not approach our education this practically, but the Wrangler debate on the immorality of capitalists was clearly theoretical because while not many of us actually paid our own way through college, most of us had by necessity to participate in that system through summer jobs, and many of us worked during the school year. I worked so many different places that I soon learned my social security number by heart long before it was common to do so.

When I first got to Rockhurst, there wasn't much call for my services. As newcomers to Kansas City, barracks boys had no contacts except the upperclassmen, who had jobs and were holding on to them, so we started looking at the help-wanted cards posted on the bulletin board opposite the dean's office in Conway Hall. Some were too far away; some required more hours than we could spare or skills that we didn't feel confident enough to fake. One looked ideal because it was confined to Saturdays and because we could apply in a group. It turned out to be door-to-door promotion of some kind of scheme that vaguely resembled green stamps or bonus bucks, and my whole group was hired.

I don't think the two men in charge could be called business or professional leaders—even we could see through their attempts to seem sophisticated, and we certainly didn't want to imitate them—but they did broaden our geographic knowledge of greater Kansas City. Once we went to Independence, Missouri and fanned out through tree-lined streets trying to give coupons to suspicious middle-aged housewives. Another time we were dropped off in Prairie Village—Pregnant Village, it was called in those days of the baby boom—where the houses and yards looked much rawer and there seemed to be no trees at all.

Meanwhile, Florian Muckenthaler, who kept a sensible distance from our follies, found a night job as dispatcher for a trucking firm. That made him a lot more money and kept him out of trouble. Some of the upperclassmen worked in a clothing store. My classmate on probation had retired from armed robbery, but another was such an accomplished shoplifter that once he lifted six cans of beer in a large drug store. I was watching him, and I thought he had only got two cans. He liked to travel with me because I had sharp features and quick movements, and clerks focused on me and ignored him.

The promotional job didn't pay very well, but it wasn't very demanding and we got a good deal of exercise. It didn't last very long, either because the campaign ended or because we got tired of the routine. Later—I can't remember the year—I went out on a solo venture to solicit contacts for a firm that enclosed front porches with louvered windows. That produced no results at all, and I realized that my father's ability as a salesman wasn't genetically transmitted.

But sales jobs were more plentiful than any other kind, and somehow—probably through my roommate's enterprise—I was hired as temporary Christmas help at Goldman's Jewelry store in downtown Kansas City. This was not easier on the feet—standing in one place is harder than walking from door to door—but at least potential customers came to me with some motivation. Of course, I could see that I didn't look like the regular staff. Think about jewelry stores—not the ones on Fifth Avenue featuring incredible buys in gold chains straight off the owner's neck or the ones in the mall attached to a discount store, but the real, old-time ones that have been there for thirty years and will be there for thirty more. The staff looks calm, respectable, solid.

I wasn't allowed near the diamonds, and I didn't have much opportunity to make valuable contacts with the permanent staff. I was seventeen and even then an obvious type-A personality, but behind a display case full of the cheaper watches and pieces of jewelry, I functioned well enough. I even managed to maintain my composure when my father showed up one day. He may have been pleased or surprised to see me imitating an adult. (He maintained this attitude until I was well past thirty and had published my first book.) After that unexpected encounter, the most demanding dowager couldn't intimidate me.

The best thing about the job at Goldman's, though, was being in downtown Kansas City. That was exciting enough at any time, but the Christmas season was special. At noon I would go to Macy's for a chef's salad, the first I had ever seen, and for the rest of lunch break and after work I would look in windows and walk down aisles full of things I had never seen before. It was like walking through the movie version of the Montgomery Ward's catalog, with better props and set design and a live cast of very well-turned-out women. Neither the merchandise nor the women seemed obtainable, but since I never expected to be able to take any of them home with me, I didn't feel frustrated or envious.

I enjoyed the Goldman's job, and I was sorry when the season ended and I had to look for another. I was especially sorry when I contrasted it with the job I got: selling women's shoes on Troost Avenue between Thirty-first and Linwood. There I began to discover that while almost nothing is as easy as it looks, most things are as bad as they sound. Unless you have a foot fetish, selling shoes ranks only a little ahead of building barbed-wire fences.

The shoe store aimed at the middle and lower-middle market, and the clientele was mostly middle-aged (thirty and over), came by public transportation, and arrived at the store after completing a number of other errands on foot. I assume that even foot fetishists make some distinctions.

The job was bearable only because it could be turned into a game. It was a challenge to put a woman into a pair of shoes that actually fit her—every 7½C wanted to wear a 5A. And the management offered incentives: awful styles would have a B stamped on the box, and you got a bonus for selling one of those. Really awful styles, stamped with a V, got you an even bigger bonus. Accessories, like clips and bows, also carried a bonus, and experienced clerks would load a shoe to double its weight and practically dare the customer to denude it.

I didn't meet any business leaders there either, but the other clerks came from different schools and backgrounds, and hanging out with them gave me a new perspective and a whole lot of new jokes. One of my colleagues was Jewish, and each was the first of his denomination the other had met. I didn't learn much about Judaism, but he learned that when Catholic girls went to confession, they did not have to reveal the names of their sexual partners. This misconception had acted as a deterrent, and I felt a little guilty about dispelling it.

One evening, as we were closing, he said that he had a date and asked if I wanted to go along. I didn't have a date or even an official girlfriend at the time, but I thought a moment and called a classmate of the girl I had dated the first semester. She agreed to go, and my colleague was impressed. We went somewhere to dance and have a beer, and after a while the women went to the ladies' room. He went to the men's room and returned, several shades paler. The wall between the two was thin, and he had heard the girls discussing their dates. I never did get him to reveal what they said.

I stuck with that job until the onset of the Easter vacation, when I first made the connection, obvious enough in the Gospel accounts, between Passover and Holy Week. This was the big season for sales, but as the manager put it, all of the Jews in the store went Orthodox. Therefore he was relying on me to work a lot of hours and, from my point of view, forfeit my own vacation. Even Boonville seemed preferable to the shoe store. To hell with this, I thought; I'm taking off. So I told him that my grandmother was sick—she had a cold, so I wasn't lying (Jesuit training paid off)—and went to Boonville, willingly for a change. I don't know if I quit at that point, but I don't remember going back.

My next job, I think—there were so many that I get confused—was delivering groceries for a family-owned store in the 5400 block of Troost. That was fun: I got to boom around the Rockhill area of what was then south Kansas City in a panel truck, seeing a lot of different styles of back doors and kitchens and people, mostly women, with their feet covered. But pretty soon the semester ended; the job didn't pay enough to make it worthwhile to stay in Kansas City, and anyway what you did in the summer was go home. Besides, going to summer school would have put me on the street still further away from my twenty-first birthday. So I quit that job and went home to Boonville.

During my sophomore year I was able to take advantage of the opportunities afforded by a Kansas City business firm and ascended the ladder from mere clerk to managerial status. In other words, I got a job working evenings and weekends for Driver's Laundrette at Fifty-sixth Street and Troost, which promised to do an average student's wash for ninety-five cents in its *Hawk* ad. Since I was the only one permanently on duty and had nominal supervision of the high school kid who came in to clean, I could describe myself as the night manager. On Saturdays I just worked there.

Since I held that job for a whole academic year, I got to know some of the clients. Charlie, the owner, was sandy-haired, with frown lines between his eyebrows that contrasted with his pleasant, equable nature. He was in his late thirties, but he had only recently been married for the first time to a rather shy woman who worked with him. The high school kid who came in to clean was tall, dark, and slender, proficient enough at his job, and quite pleasant.

Charlie was easy to work for, but then nothing much happened to irritate him. Despite the jokes about car dealers, my father had raised me to give an honest count, and the job was not demanding: weigh the dirty clothes and charge by the pound; give advice about the sorting of clothes and the use of machines when asked; give assistance when things went wrong (usually too much detergent in the machines or clothes that got tangled in the dryers). Customers who left their bundles to be washed, dried, and folded at so much extra per pound were even easier to deal with because they went away. There was even a little entertainment value in looking for lipstick on men's shorts—inside laundry joke—and in practical experience with the mechanics of women's lingerie. Names occasionally proved difficult. One night a customer dropped off a bundle. "And what is the name, sir?" "Rape." "I beg your pardon?" "Rape." "How do you spell that, sir?" "R-A-P-E." "Very good, sir." In later years a friend remarked that on occasion I assumed the role of a "very proper butler." This was where I learned it.

All sorts of people wandered in. Most were pleasant or anonymous, though one fairly busy night a tipsy woman with a somewhat cowed husband tried to monopolize all of the dryers and, when I prevented her, threatened to have my job. "Ma'am," I replied, "if you can have my job, you're welcome to it." I stole that line, but it was effective.

Only two people hung around often enough to talk to me about anything but laundry. One was a Christian Scientist with (I think) multiple sclerosis. I came to understand his slurred way of speaking, though I never did grasp his philosophical arguments. He was interested in the rudimentary Aristotelian Thomism I was beginning to absorb from my philosophy courses as well as the Catholic theology that overlaid it. He was the first non-Catholic with whom I had ever discussed these matters and the first severely disabled person I had talked to at all.

The other visitor was a black man who worked at the service station catty-corner from the laundrette. Kansas City was not officially segregated, but one didn't see many blacks above Twenty-third Street, even at officially unsegregated Rockhurst. I was a little wary about discussing racial problems, but one night he told me that he had grown up in St. Louis. He had come to Kansas City for a visit, realized that blacks were a hell of a lot better off in this semiwestern town than in semisouthern St. Louis, and gone back only to pick up his clothes. I felt pleased that he was pleased, some local pride in his endorsement, and some personal pride in his being willing to tell me this.

Mostly, though, there weren't a lot of people around at night. I could talk to K. on the pay phone by the door or read textbooks or other material that was not too demanding. By the second semester, when I established a rhythm—working, studying, writing for the *Hawk*, and dating—my grades improved dramatically.

When my sophomore year ended, I was sorry to leave the laundrette, but once again, the job couldn't pay enough for room and board as well as incidental expenses, and I couldn't expect Charlie to hold the job for me over the summer.

The job I held for most of my junior year at the drugstore on the northwest corner of Fifty-fifth and Troost didn't pay any worse than the laundromat, but I enjoyed it a lot less. For one thing, though nothing was complicated, I was supposed to do a lot of different things: open cartons, stock shelves, and wrap feminine hygiene products in dull, marbled green paper; clerk at the tobacco and notions counter on the south side of the store; work the soda fountain on the north side of the store; give minor assistance as required to the pharmacists behind the high counter on the west side of the store.

I didn't really mind any of this, though I was never comfortable behind the soda fountain. The problem was the owner, a large woman with a penetrating voice and brusque manner who wasn't a pharmacist. I had heard—from my mother, primarily—that it was harder to work for a woman than for a man, and this boss did nothing to undercut the stereotype. What we had was a failure to communicate. I was used to my father's style of management. He would say, "Do this"—actually, "While you're resting, go out and . . ."—and didn't care how long it took as long as it got done, which it did, or else. Therefore, I was used to judging my performance by the results, and because I moved faster than most people, I would finish a job quickly and sit down. She didn't seem to notice results; she defined work as looking busy, which seemed pointless to me and still does. We never quite resolved this conflict, but it didn't get heated enough for her to fire me or for me to quit.

Otherwise, it wasn't a bad job. I got a discount on cigarettes and discovered that carrying a pack of Spuds (menthol cigarettes that lost out to Kools) would discourage most hardened cadgers. The store carried liquor, and though I was legally too young to sell it and did so only when everyone else was busy, I could certainly ring it up after hours and take it back to the barracks to stash for a dance or party.

This was illegal, but by then I understood the Jesuit distinction between the illegal and the immoral. Selling condoms was clearly immoral—using them was an unthinkable compounding of the sin of fornication—and customers had to wait until one of the pharmacists was free to sell them a package of Trojans from the stock behind the counter.

Sometimes, after closing, I would sit in the back with the older, crustier pharmacist and the other part-time worker, a pharmacy student from Kansas City University, and have a few drinks. The pharmacist waited until he had finished filling prescriptions to open a bottle. He never said much, but the other student and I would chat. We had some things in common, but despite the proximity of our schools, we never saw each other outside the drugstore. Work was work and school was school, and I was a little uncomfortable when Rockhurst contemporaries came into the store, not because I thought they would scorn me for being in trade but because separate worlds were mingled and confused.

That was not a problem in my senior year because none of my contemporaries could see what I was doing. In fierce competition, I got a Saturday job as janitor's helper in the central office of a firm that manufactured air conditioners for buildings. I got the job less on my merits than on the recommendation of the Rockhurst dean's secretary, for whom I had always had a pleasant word even when I was waiting to be called on the carpet. In fact, that was the most valuable lesson I learned about contacts: always be nice to secretaries.

The job paid well by the standards of the time, and the work was so routine that I could think about something else while performing it. When I mastered the not very complicated technique of controlling the machine, buffing the long hall was particularly soothing, and once while doing this I blocked out a short story that received honorable mention in a contest and has fortunately not survived. My supervisor was satisfied with my work, though once when I showed up with a raging hangover, he put me to scraping paint, and he was pleased at the notion that I was going on to better things because I didn't regard this work as beneath me. (In the 1970s, when college radicals tried to identify with the working class, a particularly earnest student pointed down the hall to the custodian and said, "Don't despise that man because of the work he does!" "Hell, no," I said, "I used to *do* that.")

This job left me with a lot of time on my hands during the week, and my friend and co-conspirator Jim Scott got me on as a colleague on the staff of the house organ for a noncollegiate sorority. I had to compose left-to-right captions listing people in the photos and make them come out flush left and right, which is a lot harder than it sounds. The editor, Jim, and I were the only males in the office, and before long there was a purge and all three of us were terminated. I didn't mind, because this was not my idea of journalism, and the janitor's job was quieter and more lucrative.

Besides, by then I was moonlighting, every other week, as makeup man for the shop that printed the *Hawk*. I remembered enough from my year at the *Cooper County Record* to align, justify, and lock in the type without any problems. The shop was quiet—I worked nights, after everyone had gone home—and I could move at my own pace. If I wanted to take a break for a pork tenderloin sandwich at a nearby diner, no one objected. And as compositor as well as editor, I could catch anything the young Turks on the staff tried to slip by me. A poem beginning "I recall the whimsical wails of whales," composed by a sophomore who is now a professor at a leading Jesuit university, got into type that went down the hellbox. So, I notice in looking at that year's file of the newspaper, did the ends of some sentences. But they disappeared in a good cause: the paper never had to pay overset charges and wound up in the black for the first time in memory. I enjoyed the work because I could use the only fine motor skill I ever acquired—now, of course, made obsolete by new technology. The equipment I used has gone to the Smithsonian, specialized antique shops, and a few small private presses.

I can't say that Rockhurst gave me invaluable contacts with business and professional leaders in Kansas City, but then again, I can't claim to have sought them out because I had no ambitions to join them in the great enterprise of American commerce. My part-time work gave me some pocket money, kept me from screwing around (in the 1950s sense of sloth, not lechery) any more than I did, and taught me that city folks in the working class and petit bourgeoisie weren't any smarter or more ingenious than people I had known in Boonville. I was well on my way—encouraged by some of my professors and colleagues—to becoming an intellectual snob, but I was never tempted by social snobbery because my various jobs helped me to remember where I came from.

Besides, I came out of college knowing how to do laundry, put together a sandwich, wash dishes, and clean floors and toilets. The intellectual training at Rockhurst was undeniably sexist, but the skills I had developed through my invaluable contacts were androgynous. And they have been useful for creating goodwill or, depending on the vicissitudes of life, in taking care of myself.

Touching Home

The prototypical act of the modern intellectual is his abstracting himself from his family.

—*Lionel Trilling*

The fact that I was doing blue collar work while trying to become a cosmopolitan intellectual did not seem anomalous. For one thing, I had grown up doing literal shit work, cleaning out cattle barns. For another, I was doing it in Kansas City, which was not Boonville. Finally, my family's strongest article of faith is that work is as interesting as the person doing it. A few years later, Grandpa Murray took over the job as clerk in a liquor store I gave up to return to graduate school, and Dad took over his job as a traveling salesman for Schwinn bicycles.

But even when I wanted—very badly—to get rid of my provincial accent and attitude, I could never quite forget where

I came from. This was useful as a spur to keep me moving forward, but it was also part of my life.

As for my family, I now realize that the ties were so strong that I didn't need to think about them. I come from a line of very independent people who seem to enjoy new situations, and it is hard to have a really good memory and be nostalgic at the same time, so I was never homesick for a town I had wanted for years to put behind me. Even in my freshman year, I went home infrequently and, after one or two exchanges of the laundry box, shoved it into a closet and found a laundromat. I suppose that I wrote to my parents and my mother wrote to me, but not very often, and while long-distance telephone calls were not impossible, in those days they were looked upon as frivolous except in emergencies. They knew where I was, and I knew where they were, and that satisfied everyone.

But occasionally, less frequently as my social life got more complicated, I would go home for a weekend. Usually I traveled this way: caught the Troost streetcar at Fifty-third; transferred to the Thirty-first Street trolley line and rode to the end of the line; walked across to where Linwood Avenue turned into U.S. 40; put down my suitcase with the Rockhurst sticker facing traffic; and stuck out my thumb.

This worked pretty well until a man named Billy Cook— an alumnus of the Missouri Training School for Boys in Boonville who had absorbed the wrong kind of training— murdered a series of people who gave him rides. That gave hitchhiking a bad name, and though drivers relaxed after a while, the business of getting free rides never really recovered. After that, and even before if the weather was bad, I took the Troost car to Linwood and caught the Greyhound at the midtown station a few blocks west.

I started to say that I went home to Boonville, but in fact "home" and "Boonville" got farther and farther apart in my mind. Of course, town and city were less than three hours apart by car, and members of my family sometimes came to Kansas City. I wouldn't have minded if they had visited me at Rockhurst, because while I was sheepish about admitting that I came from Boonville, it never occurred to me to be ashamed of my family. In fact, when I quoted one of my grandfather's (Republican) political opinions to Father Mac and he sniffed at the views of a Missouri farmer, I replied with unexpected heat that my grandfather, who had served as state legislator in both Kansas and Missouri, had a good deal of practical political experience. If Grandpa Murray could have ignored Father Mac's Roman collar and Father Mac could have ignored Grandpa's Republican affiliation, they might have gotten on well. Even if they hadn't, the encounter would have been fun to watch. But no adult from my family visited Rockhurst between the time when my mother dropped me off and when my immediate family came to my graduation.

When family members did come to Kansas City, I would meet them somewhere else, and it was interesting to see them on neutral turf. During my freshman year, Grandpa came to be examined for a possible hemorrhoid operation, and I went to visit him, dispensed from the usual freshman curfew. The place turned out to be more like a hotel than a hospital, and we sat in his room drinking whiskey—straight bourbon, since one of his few articles of faith was that blended whiskey was an abomination—and talking until well into the night. I don't remember what we talked about, or more likely what he talked about—probably he told highly exaggerated anecdotes and delivered eccentric political opinions, because that is what he always did.

Somewhat later, both he and my father were in town on different business errands, and we met at a midtown hotel and shared a bottle of whiskey and talked. Technically this was a three-way conversation, but Dad wasn't easy for me to talk to, and he liked listening to Grandpa, which is why they got on well. I don't remember the content of that talk either, but I do remember the tone and rhythm and my sense that I was being initiated into adult male society, of being taught by men and with men in a very different sense from the language of the Rockhurst brochure.

Dad came to Kansas City fairly often for the dealers' auto auction, but that was a day trip. Sometimes he would call me to drive a purchase back to Boonville, but the only time he came to see me was at Goldman's Jewelry, well out of his usual path. He wasn't much for small talk, and after a few minutes he said, "Do you get an employee discount?" I did. "How much?" I told him—25 percent, I think. "Get yourself a good watch. I'll pay for it." (I got a Bulova that ran almost fourteen years before I had it oiled or cleaned and still does when I wind it.) Having concluded his errand, he left.

Once Mom came to Kansas City with my younger brother's junior high school basketball team, and K. and I went to the game, mostly because she wanted to meet my mother. They seemed to get along all right, but I was clearly not included in the conversation, nor did I want to be. I watched the basketball game, which the Boonville contingent lost handily.

During my senior year, my brother, then fifteen, came up to be taken to the NAIA basketball tournament and see the sights. I couldn't introduce him to a room full of coeds, but I did take him to the Nelson Art Gallery, which I had probably discovered through feminine influence. The door we entered opened on modernist art, and I thought I was going to have to tackle him to keep him from running off in panic. But before long we found a Renaissance painting—Michelangelo?—and I had a hard time getting him to look at anything else. I was pleased with his visit because it was the first time we seemed to enjoy the same things and because I could do some initiating of my own.

Sometimes I was reminded that the family constituted more than the Boonville branch. During the summer of 1952 my mother wanted to get out of town herself. Dad had become increasingly hard to budge except by business or periodic drinking bouts, so I got to accompany her. Traveling with Mom was less a trip than an adventure because she was curious about almost everything and delighted by almost everything she learned. She and I drove to Albuquerque—my first visit since 1939—to stay with Aunt Cary, my father's older sister who, because of the crippling arthritis of Nanelou Sweeney, their half-sister, had become unofficial and highly effective matriarch of the extended family. Her children—one an architect, one an engineer, neither a model for someone not inclined toward math—were adults, too old to be interested in me, and the first grandchildren were too young. But Cary told good stories about the family and seemed to know every Anglo, most Hispanics, and some Indians across the whole of New Mexico. She was involved in a complicated and enjoyable wrangle with a sheep-herder who occupied forty acres she owned east of Albuquerque, half of it flat, half at a forty-five degree angle, which seemed to me too steep and barren to worry about.

Cary was a good tour guide because she was as curious and enthusiastic as my mother and had a vast fund of odd information about everything and everyone she saw or remembered. She took us to Santa Fe: the plaza, winding narrow streets lined by adobe walls, not a bit like the Country Club Plaza in Kansas City; a restaurant where I had my first trout, which was more troublesome and less tasty than I imagined; the bar at La Fonda, where I had my first Carta Blanca beer.

(Nearly thirty years later, I drove two of my children to Albuquerque, and Cary took us to Santa Fe. They were too young for the Carta Blanca, but the trip gave me a satisfying sense of continuity.)

She also took Mom and me to a dance at a pueblo, where for the first time I felt uncomfortable not because of what I was doing but of who and where I was. To someone raised in Missouri, the corn seemed pitifully short and meager, and the dancing even more monotonous and far less comprehensible than the Latin ritual of Sunday mass. I didn't feel superior, and unlike some visitors to New Mexico I never had the illusion that I could be an Indian or anything but what I was, even if I didn't know what that meant. I did feel like a voyeur because I could see that the dance was serious business, not a spectacle for tourists, and I felt some resentment at the Indians for letting me watch and some guilt at the poverty that caused them to do so. At seventeen, I didn't realize that they might have very complicated feelings about me, but encountering something totally alien was probably good for me.

Almost as alien was the bar in Dalhart, Texas, the only place open to provide Mom's coffee fix at 10:00 A.M. on the drive back, where Hispanic males in their undershirts sat at the bar drinking beer out of bottles. Mom didn't even blink; she had been in rougher places during Prohibition and she was used to Dad. It was the best coffee I had ever tasted.

We were headed toward Wichita, another Davis clan site, to pick up our share of the family furniture stored after Nanelou had to go into a nursing home. We hitched a rental trailer to the car and had to back it up to the loading dock. I don't remember whether Mom failed or—in view of her character, unlikely—refused even to try, but at some point she turned the wheel over to me and I made it on the first try. I knew that this was blind luck, but I tried not very successfully to act casual and to conceal some of my pleasure and relief.

Looking back, I can see that the trip complemented the whiskey in my father's Kansas City hotel room, giving me a glimpse of adult status and privileges from the female side of the family. I still didn't understand the responsibilities or the means of carrying them out, but it was clear that the men and women of my family assumed that I would be able to.

Later I made a solo visit to Wichita to visit Aunt Nanelou, who had taken me on my first trip to New Mexico at the age of four and had sent marvelous books at Christmas and birthdays ever since. She had gone to live with my uncle Gough and his large family. I caught the train at Union Station, carrying a translation of Thucydides (I think; I know it had a blue cover with white printing) that Father Mac had loaned me to try to improve my mind. I had hardly opened it when several University of Kansas coeds got on the train at Lawrence and filled the seats next to and across from me. I felt awe at their big-school sophistication, but I managed to conceal that. (Thucydides may have had a similar effect on them, though this use of history would have dismayed Father Mac.) We chatted about this and that for the rest of the trip. One offered me a ride, but my uncle had arranged to meet me.

Everyone in the family knew and had come to accept the fact that he and Dad did not get along, and I hadn't seen him often enough to recognize him easily even if he had been there, which he wasn't. So I put down my bag and lit a cigarette, figuring that if he didn't find me, I could take a cab. Then I heard a voice eerily like my father's say, "When did you start smoking those damned things?" I turned and saw a man who looked like a compressed version of my father, shorter and wider, looking at me as if he expected to be disappointed.

What the hell, I had been put down by experts. "I'm sorry you had to come down," I said. "Some girls from KU offered to give me a ride anywhere I needed to go."

He looked at me more warily and grumbled, "Just like your old man." This was obviously not intended as a compliment, but since I had never before been compared with my father, I was quite pleased. (Later, though, I said something about taking inorganic chemistry to get into the oil business, and, a promoter himself, he got to point out that oil was organic. We tacitly agreed to settle for a standoff.)

At his large and well-furnished house, I spent some time talking to my aunt, whose mind was far more agile than her body, and trying to sort out my numerous cousins. The oldest happily announced that he had challenged a friend with a brother in high school to a basketball game in the driveway. I had visions of an all-city hotdog, but the brother was slow and unathletic, and we demolished them. My cousin doesn't remember that, but one of his younger sisters recalls my teaching her to play "Chopsticks." Over the years, our generations have turned out to share a good many traits and interests, and the family feud died where it began, with our fathers.

Mostly, though, family meant the people in Boonville, and my visits home were not always as productive or interesting as those to Albuquerque and Wichita. I was convinced that my father didn't understand me, but since I wasn't always pleased with myself, I wasn't sure I wanted him to, and I was quite certain that it was not only unjust but unsafe to try to condescend to him.

When I got home, my mother would ask about what I was doing, and my father would listen and sometimes make a gruff response. I would say hello to my brother and sister, five and ten years younger, but we wouldn't have much to talk about. I would go across the big backyard to say hello to my grandmother, who would ask if I wanted something to eat and try not to say that I looked thin, and listen to my grandfather on the folly of the Truman administration or whatever happened to annoy or interest him at the moment.

Otherwise, there wasn't much to do on weekends. I would stop by Foster's Drug Store to say hello to Frank Foster if he was on duty. Ray McKinzie and I and whoever else happened to be around—most of my high school class had left town—would go across the Missouri River to the Hacienda for a few beers. Sunday morning I would see older and soberer people at mass. Some time after dinner at noon, I would catch the Greyhound back to Kansas City and return to the barracks. Even though they were shabby and cramped and the local food was even worse than my mother's cooking, I was always glad to be back. Kansas City wasn't home, but it was where I lived.

Christmas and other school breaks were in some ways better than weekends because friends from other colleges were around and because, during weekdays, I could visit adults whose example and concern I valued, like Jessie Dedrick at the public library, one of the few people in town to whom I could talk about books, and E. J. Melton at the *Cooper County Record*, who had taught me most of what little I knew about writing. But after we exchanged the usual pleasantries, there wasn't much to talk about. After a day or two, I was ready to go back to Kansas City.

Summer vacations were in almost every way worse because they went on so long that I couldn't even pretend that I wasn't living in Boonville. Looking back forty years, I can see that in physical terms, Boonville wasn't much more limited than the Rockhurst neighborhood where I spent most of my time. It had three drugstores within walking distance, but downtown Boonville had more than that, and Foster's had a larger and more varied stock than any of those along Troost Avenue. Craig's was smaller than the Country Club Dairy where barracks freshmen took their evening break, but the ice cream was at least as good.

The Hacienda didn't have shuffleboard, but it had a more homey atmosphere than Leo's Blatz Tavern across the Kansas line. Boonville had two movie theaters that each changed features once a week and a new drive-in, and while they didn't show anything avant-garde, it took me more than a year to develop a taste for foreign films. The public library wasn't as big as the college library, but it had enough books to further my education if I had been interested. (Once I checked out a volume of Nietzsche, and though I didn't read it, I did learn to spell his name.) Boonville didn't have museums and other cultural attractions, but I couldn't claim to miss these because I had rarely visited any of the ones in Kansas City.

Many of my Boonville friends were smarter or funnier or more ambitious or all three than the ones I surrounded myself with my first year at Rockhurst, and with the exception of Jim Scott, I have stayed in closer touch with them than with anyone I knew at Rockhurst. One, now an architect, had better jokes, a wilder sense of humor, and a far wider knowledge of contemporary jazz than anyone I knew in Kansas City. Others were capable of carrying on serious conversations about questions of life and conduct that somehow didn't arise in the barracks, or at least in my presence.

But even with these friends I had begun to realize that in Boonville I was merely marking time. In theological terms, it wasn't Limbo, because that was reserved for the unbaptized who were perfectly happy because they didn't know what they were missing. It wasn't even Purgatory because there, at least, souls were expiating temporal punishment due to sins committed during earthly life and the prayers of the faithful on earth could earn them good time and an early out. I knew what I was missing, and no outside intervention was going to shorten my sentence.

Anyway, that's the way I felt about it then. Like most earthly prisoners, I was convinced that I didn't deserve to be there. Clearly I didn't belong. At the beginning of my first summer back home, I stopped to see Mr. Melton at the *Record*. Although a new secretary-receptionist-bookkeeper sat at the desk, the office smelled reassuringly familiar and everything else was in its accustomed place. Obviously I was not because the first thing he said was that he didn't have a job for me. At seventeen I had become accustomed to rejection, but now I was being rejected for something I hadn't even asked for.

On the other hand, I did need a job, not just for the money but for self-respect and for something to do. After a few days, Dad got me hired at the Missouri Farmers Association grain elevator, and that took care of my days and some Saturdays. The men I worked with were laborers, not the kind of people I was used to associating with even in Boonville, but they were pleasant enough to me, and it was more relaxing to be around them than the jewelry clerks and shoe salesmen and advertising hustlers I had worked with in the city because I didn't have to pretend to be a member of the commercial classes.

The work was physically hard. When I wasn't unloading feed sacks from boxcars I was loading them on to ton-and-a-half trucks; and when I wasn't shoveling wheat out of farm trucks I was nailing up boxcars for shipping it somewhere else; and at odd moments I tested cream in a small room where open gas flames under the vats for washing cans raised the temperature and humidity even higher than the rest of central Missouri. But it built muscle if not character, and it was there, closed up in a boxcar and drenched in sweat, that I received the revelation that I wanted to be a member of the professional class.

Twice a week, as I had the previous summer, I played city league softball for the Catholic Youth Organization team. Nominally it was fast pitch, but only one pitcher in the league had much speed or stuff. Every third baseman shifted toward short for left-handed batters, and I could lay down a bunt off a medium-speed pitch and practically walk to first base. Our coach, who knew less about softball than I do about astrophysics, seemed to think that if it wasn't a full swing, it didn't count, but I hit over .400 for the season and, after we did happily without a coach, for as long as I played. We didn't finish first that year or any other, but we won often enough to stay interested.

Although I despised the saying "It isn't whether you won or lost, but how you played the game," I have to admit, in enforced retirement, that he had a point. Between the foul lines or in the batter's box, I knew the territory, the rules, the strategy, and the consequences of every action. The sudden, explosive release of tension in swinging the bat to make contact, breaking toward second in an attempted steal, shifting weight to grab a grounder in the infield or straightening to make a controlled sprint to settle under a fly ball in the outfield—these movements had a completeness and purity that an aging man can have only in the joy and pain of kinetic memory. But at the time, of course, I didn't think about moving; I just did it.

Unlike Klusemeyer's Alley Rats, the outlaw baseball team I had played for in high school composed of various religions, races, and social classes, the softball team was made up of people whom I had seen every day for years in school and church. But when the game ended, my more sober teammates went their own ways and the less sober ones met me at the Hacienda or some other haven for underage drinkers.

If I didn't think about playing ball, I didn't think about much of anything that summer, and though I probably read some books, I can't remember any titles. I already knew that I would rather be in college than unloading boxcars, though I was vain enough to be glad that the work strengthened my muscles and broadened my shoulders. Morally it was useful because it gave me more respect for people who did manual labor and enough knowledge of them to recognize their limitations. And I had more respect for myself because I had worked hard.

The summer after my sophomore year was far less satisfactory because I left a lot more behind me in Kansas City. My academic standing had improved—all A's, except for biology, in a semester in which I took nineteen hours, worked twenty hours a week, carried on what was, by the standards of Catholics in 1952, a passionate romance, and had become associate editor in my second semester on the *Hawk*.

Back in Boonville my father hired me as gofer on the used car lot he ran with Sam Jewett. Working for my father was never easy, but this job wasn't hard. I washed and vacuumed cars, moved them around the lot as needed, and stalled potential customers if both Dad and Sam were otherwise occupied. The most exciting part of the job was going to the dealers' auction in Kansas City, watching Dad compete in the big time, and drive back one of his purchases. But the auction was far north of my home territory, and the surroundings (concrete floors, plastic sofa covers, oil stains) were not inspiring.

Mostly, however, I sat in a trailer in front of a wholly inadequate fan and stared north on Main Street. I tried to read *Crime and Punishment* but gave up after thirty pages because I thought my situation even more desperate and a good deal hotter than Raskolnikov's. Several times a day I walked over to the Conoco station on the corner to get a coke from the machine and bullshit with Marshall Best, who wasn't exactly the manager but wasn't exactly not. The high point of the working day was lying to the occasional Yankee tourist—Main Street was also U.S. Highway 40, the major east-west route—about how cool it was for this time of year.

I wrote interminable and, when I didn't have my typewriter, illegible letters to K. in her hometown some two hundred miles away and waited for her replies in flawless penmanship that she could vary according to her mood. I have no idea what we wrote about, and I don't think I really want to know.

One weekend my father allowed me to use a car to visit K. Aside from the five flat tires and a total-out wreck (a grasshopper crawled down my shirt-front and distracted me), the weekend was not entirely disastrous. It began with my visit to Monsignor Roels, pastor of my parish during most of my years at Boonville Catholic High School, now in semiretirement as chaplain of the Catholic hospital in K.'s hometown. I owed him more than I could articulate; he was a bit ironic about what the Jesuits were doing to me. I asked for his blessing, which I certainly needed. The effects didn't last long, and my intimacy with K. escalated to a stage that today would be regarded as innocent and clinically safe but disturbed us morally as much as it excited us physically.

The rest of the summer was anticlimactic. My father lamented the reduction in inventory occasioned by the wreck—"I could have made some money on that car"—but he always dealt better with major screw-ups than with misdemeanors, perhaps because this was one area in which he could identify with me. At any rate, when he drove with me to deal with the prosecuting attorney and dispose of possible charges against me as a result of the accident, he talked to me more easily and frankly than usual. Again, I don't remember what he said. Perhaps teenage boys are like dogs, responding to tone rather than to content.

The summer of 1954 was the worst I could remember. Until I started writing this book and glanced at a popular history of the period that to me wasn't history but my life, I didn't know that America was in a recession. If I had known it then, I might have felt less frustrated about not finding a job. It wasn't so much the lack of income as a lack of coherence. I even went back to Kansas City to make rounds with an encyclopedia salesman, but I obviously hadn't gotten any better at door-to-door sales since my freshman year. His practiced cynicism was momentarily impressive but not, with a little reflection, worth trying to copy, and Rockhurst in the summer wasn't any more exciting than Boonville, so I went home where at least I didn't have to pay room and board.

One week Dad got me a job plowing corn in the Missouri River bottoms. That was hotter and far less interesting than the grain elevator because there was no one to talk to, and if your mind wanders, so does the tractor, which doesn't do the corn a bit of good. There were odd jobs around the home place, feeding stock and stacking hay in the barn.

But these chores didn't occupy much time; and perhaps to do some local service but mostly to get me out of the house, Dad started volunteering my services to local organizations.

My week as counselor to a troop of local boy scouts at a camp on the Lake of the Ozarks was one of the low points not just of a bad summer but of my life. I still won't watch movies about summer camp. Twelve- and thirteen-year-olds are natural smart alecks, and I had no knowledge of how to deal with them and even less sympathy for their vagaries. My group was composed entirely of stragglers, and I spent my days trying to herd them to and through various activities. On the day they tried to pass the test for their merit badge on tree identification, one sorted through his finds, identifying them as he handed them to me: pin oak, jack oak, post oak, poison ivy. I did earn a measure of respect during a semiofficial pillow fight by decking another counselor with a borrowed weapon that one of my troop had loaded with a blunt object. I was glad that I didn't hurt him—he was a refreshing contrast to the professional scouters, who seemed resolutely cheerful, stuffily pious about the values of their organization, and depressingly reluctant to head for the nearest tavern when we finally put our charges to sleep.

My experience as assistant coach of the American Legion baseball team was more enjoyable, partly because I had never had a regular starting position in my years on the team and partly because I knew more about baseball than the nominal manager, who soon disappeared, so that I got to run things my own way. Not that my knowledge did the team much good; it was outgunned by other Legion teams, all drawn from much larger populations. The most talented members of the team were three catchers, and, inspired by the example of the Brooklyn Dodger manager who moved Gil Hodges to first base and Bruce Edwards to third when Roy Campanella came along, I moved them around. One was too slow to be anything but a catcher but fancied himself a base-stealing threat. One was quick, so I put him at second base, thus annoying the father of the incumbent, whom I moved to the outfield because he couldn't field ground balls very well. I forgot what I did with the third. Perhaps he was the left fielder who passed out from the heat one Sunday afternoon. My only link with writing was calling in box-scores to the Columbia *Tribune*. I remember winning only one game, but everyone survived the season.

Other than that, things were pretty grim. I had broken up with K. through fear of eternal damnation and of permanent entanglement, so I didn't even have letters to read and write. Once or twice I went out with women—older or Protestant or both—who seemed intimidatingly sophisticated and who probably associated with me because the pickings were at least as slim for college girls returned to Boonville as they were for me. Nothing much happened; we were going through the motions, like my players at infield practice. The wrong move could be momentarily embarrassing, but the score book wasn't open.

That was my last summer in Boonville for a while. During my senior year at Rockhurst, I didn't exactly look forward because I had no clear idea of what I was going to do, but I certainly didn't look back.

In the spring of 1955, Dad drove up for the father-son banquet designed to show the former how the Jesuits had educated the latter into whole men, as advertised. I was rather surprised and on the whole pleased that my father had agreed to come, and when I look at the *Hawk* story, I am even more impressed now because only about 6 percent of the potential fathers and sons turned up.

It was interesting and a little daunting to see our situations reversed. In Boonville, I was known to the adult world primarily as the son of M. C. Davis. At the banquet, he was identifiable only as the father of Bob Davis, who was not a candidate for high academic honors but was quite visible as editor of the student newspaper, winner of some literary contests, and member, with about 9,000 other people, of *Who's Who Among Students in American Colleges and Universities*—the only non-Kansas Citian of the ten from Rockhurst.

This was my world, and while I was still a bit worried about being able to live up to my father's expectations and a whole lot worried about living up to the expectations of the world represented by the fathers of the other seniors, I was even more nervous about his being able to live up to those of the immediate situation.

This reaction surprised me. After all, Dad would be forty-seven a few days after the banquet—unimaginably old. He had, I knew vaguely, been around the block and up more than one alley. He was known all over Cooper and Howard counties as a shrewd trader of cars, trucks, and cattle. He was not someone to mess with.

Here, though, I was not sure that anyone would know this, or care if they did know. As we parked at the restaurant near the Country Club Plaza, I could see that some (it seemed most) of the other cars were newer and more highly polished than the one Dad was driving, and his dealer's plates implied a certain lack of stability. Moreover, he looked out of place. It wasn't so much that the fathers from Kansas City dressed and talked differently—Dad had an eye for good clothes, and when he had nothing to say, he didn't say it, unlike his son. But he obviously belonged outdoors, not behind a desk.

Anyway, I worried less about the context of the other fathers than about that of the college faculty and staff. Other fathers might look more prosperous or more sophisticated, but the Jesuits and laymen represented the kind of people whom my parents paid to convince me to adopt values and a way of life very different from theirs. (Actually, the ones I respected were not the kind to show up at a father-son banquet, but for my immediate anxieties academics were academics.)

Things turned out all right. Dad was a salesman and could listen, unruffled, to any kind of nonsense, including this kind. The usual people made the usual noises about being glad to meet him and about the accomplishments of his son. We escaped more of that by sitting with Jim Scott and his father, who worked for Jackson County in some outdoor supervisory capacity and was even more puzzled than Dad at the ugly duckling emerging from his nest. But I was relieved when the evening was over because for the first time I felt responsible not just to but for my father.

Wise in My Generation

The true task is reconciliation with reality and the true reconciliation, Kierkegaard says, is religion.

—Donald Barthelme, "Kierkegaard Unfair to Schlegel"

There was something ineffably gorgeous somewhere that had nothing to do with God.

—F. Scott Fitzgerald, "Absolution"

The brochure doesn't have a date, but it portrays a Rockhurst College football game, the mailing address doesn't have a zone number, and most of the students pictured are wearing suits, so it is before my time. The photograph beside the caption, "Rockhurst College Answers the Eight Questions," shows a Jesuit standing at a blackboard and pointing to an arrow. Above it is "Intellect"; below it is "Will." The arrow points to a large asterisk. The caption reads "Learning the True Philosophy of Life." I don't remember what the asterisk stands for—perhaps salvation or a synonymous term like the choice of good—not because the solution is as difficult as one of Father Doyle's algebra problems but because I wasn't paying attention. Like Augustine, I wanted to be holy—but not right now.

Scott Fitzgerald and Donald Barthelme were not quite successfully lapsed Catholics from the provinces who left the church in pursuit of worldly success but never quite escaped the sense that the world had or ought to have a moral order. By 1955, I had scarcely heard of Fitzgerald, and though Barthelme came from a more cultured background than I, he had yet to write anything beyond undergraduate whimsy and movie and art reviews for the Houston *Post*.

Like Fitzgerald's heroes, I wanted the transformation of an earthly grace. It wasn't so much Gatsby's glittering things that I wanted—I had paid attention to some of the Jesuits and ignored the brochure's promises to make me into a successful business and professional man, so I wasn't worldly in that fashion—as a way of being at ease with people different in kind, not just degree, from the grownups I had seen in Boonville. I wanted to get and spend not money but sophistication.

It would have been nice to find a magic formula, like the "shazam" that transformed Billy Batson, the newsboy, into Captain Marvel, but except for *Mad*, I was past the comic book stage. I still read pulp fiction, but I no longer took it seriously, not because I despised it aesthetically but because I had decided that its methods for achieving success wouldn't work. Fitzgerald's James Gatz writes his resolutions in a copy of *Hopalong Cassidy* (a good trick, since the book hadn't been published when he dates the entry), utters "Jay Gatsby," and transforms himself; Rudolph Miller in "Absolution" renames himself "Blatchford Sarnemington" and is thwarted. As my grandfather used to say, "You have to hold your mouth right."

I couldn't get my lips around the formula on the blackboard because even if it could open a door, I didn't want to go through it. In some moods, I didn't want to have to cope with any adult version of the world, and for a long time my favorite writers were humorists and ironists—H. Allen Smith, Robert Benchley, James Thurber, some of H. L. Mencken—who used ridicule to hold the world at bay. At the time, I didn't know that this was usual for American boys from the provinces—Hemingway with Ring Lardner, Donald Barthelme with Ambrose Bierce. Like the character in Barthelme's "Kierkegaard Unfair to Schlegel" who alternates fantasies of meeting a girl on a train with philosophical discussion, I loved my irony even though it gave only a little pleasure.

But even a late adolescent could see that this was not the best way of coping with the world. For one thing, it tended to annoy the people I wanted to impress; for another, it was just a delaying tactic that allowed me to live to fight another day. (Most people my age can remember the verse about running away; I don't know anyone who remembers the first verse, which deals with staying to fight.) But to win, you had to have some offensive weapons.

In 1955, there wasn't much in anyone's arsenal. That was the year of *Rebel Without a Cause*. In fact, many people, including some of us at Rockhurst, had a cause, or at least a gripe, against the commercialized blandness of the Eisenhower era, when the secretary of defense, Engine Charlie Wilson, could say, without any sense of irony or shame, that what was good for General Motors was good for the country. After Dylan Thomas died in 1953, someone wrote, "You killed him, you sons-of-bitches in your Brooks Brothers suits," but this, like the widespread graffito "Bird Lives!" two years later, was a feeble protest rather than a counterstrike.

The search for a style pervades *The Scene Before You: A New Approach to American Culture* (1955), a collection of articles published over the previous seven years. Milton Klonsky explained the decline and fall of Greenwich Village; Arnold W. Green,

"Why Americans Feel Insecure"; Marshall McLuhan, "The Psychopathology of 'Time' and 'Life' "; Anatole Broyard, the institutionalization of hipster values. Robert Warshow examined "The Liberal Conscience in [Arthur Miller's] *The Crucible*" and decided that the play allowed the audience to "experience together the sense of their own being, their close community of right-mindedness in the orthodoxy of 'dissent.' " Chandler Brossard, who edited the collection, uttered the "Plaint of a Gentile Intellectual" who struggles with the feeling that "the Jewish intellectual is the only intellectual who is really 'hip,' that is, in the know, and that the Gentile is 'square,' or naive."

Even I knew that this was the worst possible thing you could be, and I didn't know any, or even know about any, New York Jewish intellectuals. Seymour Krim, who did, didn't speak that highly of them in "Our Middle-Aged 'Young Writers,' " who lacked the 1920s tone, "fresh, tangy, brash, and completely different in tone and point of view from the older generation. . . . Independent, vigorous, and ready to gamble, they lived up, or down, to their cocky youth." Instead, every notable member of the dominant new generation—J. D. Salinger, Saul Bellow, Eudora Welty, Paul Bowles, Mary McCarthy, Ralph Ellison—was

> sublimating his life to a specific, European-inspired, early-20th-century conception of High Art, [so that] the prevailing attitude precluded the development of a different point of view, and of different parts of the personality not thought to be of the highest value and hence either scorned or ignored. [As a result, these writers] find themselves unprepared for the life around them. . .either as writers or people. And their earlier ideals, modeled on a particular attitude, are no longer relevant, by the testimony of their own lives.

In a postscript, Krim demanded "a fiction—nay, a fact!—equal to the intellectual pace and new sense of possibility which our minds have become tuned to." In retrospect, he sounds like a

John the Baptist preparing the way for Allen Ginsberg's *Howl*, published in 1956, and Jack Kerouac's *On the Road*, a year later.

Had *Commentary* been available to me during my college days, I might have agreed with Krim. The *Americana* yearbook, not usually thought of as avant-garde, certainly did, regarding 1955 as "innocuous" in literary terms and anomalous for the Luce magazine's praise of Herman Wouk's *Marjorie Morningstar*.

New or recent books that came to my attention were as feeble as the popular music of the period. (Like most other people, I didn't learn about John Hawkes, Ralph Ellison, and Flannery O'Connor until later.) For a slightly later generation than mine, Salinger's *Catcher in the Rye* became almost a sacred text. Not to me. I found a copy on a lower shelf in the Rockhurst library stacks and read the first few pages before I stood up. I finished it out of snobbery—it was being mentioned as an important book—but I couldn't see what all the fuss was about. I hadn't been happy at Holden Caulfield's age, and I still disliked the kind of people he did. But he had a lot better deal than I did, and all he did was whine and worry about where the ducks went in the winter. I had more experience with livestock: either they migrated or someone rounded them up, fed them until it was time to turn them loose again, and shoveled out the duck shit.

As far as I know, none of my contemporaries read Salinger, but dismembered copies of James Jones's *From Here to Eternity* and Norman Mailer's *The Naked and the Dead* had a lively underground circulation in the barracks. You took any segment that was offered without regard for unity and coherence, and to this day I have no sense of the continuity of either book or for that matter of the two books as separate artifacts. But in 1955 Mailer published *The Deer Park*, the best illustration I know—since I've never even tried to read a subsequent Mailer novel—of Alexander Pope's dictum that

Obscenity with dulness still must prove
As shameful sure as impotence in love.

I have no idea what Jones was up to then or subsequently.

Of course, we didn't read these books for their literary value or even because they gave us vicarious experience of the war we had been too young to fight or because they helped us to understand the legendary race of veterans who had already passed through Rockhurst. We read them because they were hot: they dealt with frank and unashamed sexual encounters, and the characters talked dirty. This was a version of the grown-up world we didn't get from any blackboard or the official literature.

Hemingway was still read for some of the same reasons. Some people used him as a sex manual. One of K.'s friends, under the influence of *For Whom the Bell Tolls*, had "gone all the way," as we called it, and referred to the experience as "La Gloria." Most of us had the more modest ambition of being able to carry our drink as well as did Hemingway's early heroes and move as easily through distant locales. But his most recent novels were *Across the River and into the Trees*, which was bad even by the standards of the 1950s, and *The Old Man and the Sea*, which had been serialized in *Life* magazine, for God's sake!

However, as an upperclassman I began to read writers who were not yet classics and were still regarded as subversive. This was partly bravado, partly a way of distinguishing myself from the Philistines who surrounded me. For example, in my senior year, I owned the Avon edition of D. H. Lawrence's *The Virgin and the Gypsy*, with the kind of lurid cover one would expect from the Hearst organization. Another man in the dorm spotted it and asked, not quite drooling, if he could borrow it. Five minutes later he burst into my room, slammed the book on my desk, and said indignantly, "Why didn't you *tell* me it was literature?"

148

This man didn't like Aldous Huxley either, but there was never any doubt that his books were literature. During most of my undergraduate years, Huxley served as a model for me— not of style, thank heaven, though I didn't yet realize that he had a tin ear—but of sophistication. Even when his characters were diffident or unhappy, they *knew* so much. In *Antic Hay*, Theodore Gumbril gives up teaching, puts a false beard over his real erudition, and has marvelous, meaningless sex with an ur-bippy, abandons the woman who can give him pure, ideal love, and is on his way to the Continent to make a good deal of money when the novel ends. I suppose that I could see Huxley's moral point about the futility of all this, but as Evelyn Waugh wrote at roughly the time I graduated, Gumbril seemed to be having a marvelous time, and I wanted to live like that. (I did get a real beard and the stacks of student essays, both of which Gumbril leaves behind.)

Huxley taught me that there was a great deal I didn't know, that books and ideas could be exciting, and that there were more and more of them all the time. Again, cultural lag helped, and I didn't run across *Time Must Have a Stop* and *Ape and Essence* in time to spoil my enjoyment of *Brave New World* and earlier novels. But I was beginning to learn that there were fashions, or movements, in the arts and that people in that vague world kept up with them.

In some ways, that was easier for provincial undergraduates to do in the 1950s than it is now. Anthology-magazines like *Discovery*, featuring the latest writers (of the kind dismissed by Krim or included in Brossard's anthology or both), sat next to the latest Mickey Spillane on the racks at the drugstore down the street. Looking back at the files, I can't be sure that I read anything except a Kenneth Fearing poem because I had encountered him as the most accessible poet in the Sanders and Nelson anthology of modern British and American poetry and (later

John) Clellon Holmes's "The Horn" because it was about a jazz musician who topples his idol in a cutting contest and then has to deal with the consequences. I read it not for the style, which now seems turgid and pretentious in all the ways that Krim described, but because it was about jazz.

If the literary avant-garde, or whatever *Discovery* printed, did not seem very new or exciting, new styles and energy were easier for me to feel, if not describe, in the music of the period, or at least in the music I had begun to be aware of in Kansas City. In my freshman year, we mostly listened to WHB, a pop radio station that featured, besides already dated singers like Guy Mitchell and Jo Stafford, the music of new artists like the Four Aces, who disbanded in the year I graduated because their lead singer left to go solo and was never heard again, and Johnny Ray. The Aces were hearty and harmonious in songs like "(It's No) Sin" to keep loving you forever, though nothing is mentioned about touching, and "Tell Me Why" I can't stop thinking about a lost lover. Johnny Ray was lugubrious in "Cry"—you'll feel better—and "The Little White Cloud That Cried."

By my senior year, I was tuned in to radio KPRS, "Where Kansas City listens." Instead of the Four Aces, I heard Johnny Ace; instead of Johnny Ray, there was Ray Charles, who woke me from a nap by hollering like a mountain jack in "One More Time."

Not everyone had made the shift. Record companies were still making one version for the funkier market, another to be played on black stations, and another for the white market. For example, whites heard "Dance with Me Henry"; blacks heard Etta James doing "Roll with Me Henry." Jukeboxes in the raunchier places had Hank Ballard's "Work with Me Annie," which had a background of moans that were obviously sexual even to those of us who had never heard them live.

In between, the radio, less homogenized than it is today, played a wide spectrum of music across the AM band, including deep-voiced black singers like Billy Eckstine and, less often, Herb Jeffries, holdovers from the big band era who appealed to whites as well as blacks. Kansas City was a good place to hear live music: in October 1954, Chet Baker, Woody Herman, and Stan Kenton all came to town the same week. I heard a good deal of live music: Kenton every time he came to the Pla-Mor Ballroom; Coleman Hawkins and George Shearing in a little club on east Highway 40 just up the hill from where I used to start hitchhiking; Errol Garner and Dizzy Gillespie with Norman Granz's Jazz at the Philharmonic. I knew about most of these musicians—although Hawkins was a surprise—because I had heard them on the radio or on specialized jukeboxes in places like Milton's, which featured bebop and catered to the hip crowd, including the first homosexual who ever tried to pick me up because I was hanging around in the men's room. It was an understandable mistake, but I wasn't cruising; I was trying to decide whether or not I was going to throw up and wasn't going to leave until the issue resolved itself one way or the other.

There was also marvelous local talent. Jay McShann had a seven-piece band that played in clubs I could walk to. Bob Wilson had a small group in which almost everyone doubled on various instruments, including the first bass clarinet I had ever seen. Julia Lee, who didn't like to travel, played her own compositions like "Stick Out Your Can, Here Comes the Garbage Man" and "I've Got a Crush on the Fuller Brush Man" in the classier downtown bars. In a less classy place on Troost Avenue, a white woman closed her set and the bar with "Shake a Hand," walking around on top of the bar and not missing a beat when a drunk pulled down her half-slip.

None of my contemporaries, except my roommate, who seemed to have little interest in analysis and none in print, shared any of my musical tastes. That was part of the point, sometimes the whole point—to show how different and superior I was. Thus, when I couldn't find someone to go with me to a live performance, I felt pleased rather than lonely. It gave me, first, the satisfaction of realizing how pure and avant-garde my tastes were, and then the satisfaction of explaining this in print.

I had begun to define myself, or thrust myself on the attention of my contemporaries at Rockhurst and CST, as a writer. This was a gradual process that accelerated as I gained control over the columns of the *Hawk*, but it started earlier and, like many habits, innocuously.

I had never been terrified by the blank page—ignorance is wonderful—and I had looked on words as counters in a game where you could bend the rules or even make them up. Writing was fun. In my freshman year, when one innocent was sentenced to write a lengthy assignment along with the guilty for some infraction I can't remember, I filled his pages as well as mine, partly out of guilt but mostly because I was on a roll and didn't want to stop. Another time, when a roommate had an overload of correspondence from a variety of girlfriends, I answered the ones on his B list, trying to adopt his style, to see if his readers would buy the forgery. I once wrote a paper for K. as an exercise in adopting a woman's vocabulary and point of view. However, I did refuse twenty dollars to write a paper for a Rockhurst business major—not because of moral scruples or a desire to preserve my amateur standing, but because the subject was too boring to make it worth my while.

When I began to write for the *Hawk*, I discovered that writing was a way to re-create myself, to prepare, as Prufrock said, a face to meet the faces that I met. (I wish I had a dollar for every time someone in my generation quoted or thought that line.)

By my senior year, I created a persona embodied in the logo to my column, "Skull Session": a grinning, bespectacled death's head with a cigarette hanging from one side of its mouth. Sometimes I was a prig by accident. More often I was a pain in the ass by design, picking on the students at St. Teresa's, the class officers, business majors, and any other targets harmless enough to get by the censors. (I thought I was very original until, years later, I discovered Donald Barthelme's columns in the University of Houston *Cougar* and realized that the style was endemic in that period.) Writing was still a game, but a more complicated and rewarding one that allowed me to believe that I was preparing to face the larger world and to keep active when I was supposed to be doing something else—which for me has always been the definition of happiness.

Much of the feature material I wrote for the *Hawk* my senior year dealt with two subjects: music and girls. I didn't know very much about either, but nobody seemed to know any more, and having this outlet gave me a new attitude toward writing. The columns about girls—their types, how to meet them and get rid of them before being entrapped, and so on—now make me wince at their easy, pseudo-Byronic cynicism. I'm reminded of Bette Midler's response to Shelley Long's near-hysterical carping in *Outrageous Fortune*: "Gee, I bet you haven't been laid in about a year!" I hadn't been laid at all.

Although the columns about music are no less pretentious and devoid of technical expertise, I find them less distasteful because they came not just from a desire to show off but from a desire to make distinctions, to analyze, to discriminate. By the time I graduated, I couldn't always date a poem unless I knew the author's name, but I could place a saxophone solo within a year of its original recording. I had also become a racist, having made the amazing discovery that white singers ripped off and cheapened black material. But that didn't make me as mad as Bill Haley and the Comets, whose material I described in a column as "a sort of clippty-clippity beat combined with asinine lyrics and a stereotyped tenor sax solo." Unlike many of my undergraduate opinions, I am not ashamed of this one.

I also looked, fairly consciously, for ways to expand my range. I took over the job of drama critic; I wrote some book reviews; I wrote parodies of popular songs and poems ("Just a Moan on Service" was the most successful) and squibs attacking the habits of students in the lounge. I even tried to go beyond verse into poetry, as in

IMAGES

> Shadows on a dance floor—
> Shadows on a cavern wall...
> He and She discussing all
> While phantoms flicker in the door
> And out again into a world
> Gray with fog and hopelessness.
> He and She with fingers furled
> Hoping to extract a Yes
> To different questions. Who
> Will say that this sad two
> Is real, while calling shades untrue?

In defense of this effort, I should point out that I hadn't been laid at all, and probably I had broken up with K. yet again. The poem does combine the Platonic theory I had learned from Father McCallin and the sexual frustration I had learned from unlimited experience. It was my last attempt at poetry for a quarter century because, in the stops I made along the way, there wasn't any call for it.

The Whole Man

On May 29, 1955, the day of my graduation, there had been some progress since my seventeenth birthday. American diplomacy had succeeded in ending the Korean War with an uneasy truce; the American ambassador to Yugoslavia had clashed with Nikita Khrushchev over U.S. criticism of Soviet farming methods and invidious comparisons between Joseph McCarthy and the head of the Soviet secret police; and the new envoy to South Vietnam, in presenting his credentials, had pointedly ignored the nominal head of the government. There was "Another Gaza Incident." The Conservative Party in England had won an even larger majority in Parliament than in the previous election.

In domestic affairs, President Eisenhower played golf in the rain, but had not decided whether to run for a second term. However, Estes Kefauver, senator from Kentucky best known for his investigation of organized crime, had decided not to run. The Supreme Court reminded Congress of the Fifth Amendment and freed three witnesses who had refused to testify before the House Un-American Activities Committee. Congress was about to extend the draft, and the air force requested an additional $300 million to speed up production of B-52 bombers, scheduled to go on duty the following month. Statehood for Hawaii and Alaska was a dead issue. There was a "Marked Decline in Racial Bias In Far West Revealed by Study," and although there was considerable debate about the distribution and efficacy of the Salk polio vaccine, the benefits were thought to outweigh the risks.

Movies were, if not better than ever, slightly more violent. *Battle Cry, Strategic Air Command,* and *Soldier of Fortune* were in first run. Domestic violence was represented by *The Blackboard Jungle,* which brought "Rock Around the Clock" to popular attention. James Dean appeared in *East of Eden,* and Joan Collins in a British import, *The Adventures of Sadie.* Joe Breen had retired as head of the Production Code office, and Cardinal McIntyre of Los Angeles was complaining about "laxity" in films and advertising. Darryl F. Zanuck, undeterred by his 1951 prediction about the feebleness of television, replied that the industry was policing itself responsibly.

In magazine journalism, the University of Illinois had given awards to *Colliers, Saturday Evening Post, Reporter,* and, the lone survivors of the attrition of mass magazines, *Redbook* and the *New Yorker.* Robert Gorham Davis, the Columbia professor responsible for my using three names professionally, was spending a year in Austria as a Fulbright lecturer. He rejected the argument that American fiction gave Europeans a bad impression of America because they were full of "images of brutality and despair," insisting that novels are works of imagination, "adventurous and soul-searching," rather than reportage.

His opponents need not have worried about novels on the best seller list, which had dumbed down considerably since 1951. François Sagan, Robert Ruark, John P. Marquand, Mac Hyman (*No Time for Sergeants*) and Patrick Dennis (*Auntie Mame*) dominated the fiction list. In nonfiction, Norman Vincent Peale's *The Power of Positive Thinking* was in its 134th week, four weeks short of *A Man Called Peter* but more than two years ahead of *Why Johnny Can't Read*.

Literate or not, more students were seeking admission to college—30 percent of high school graduates, as opposed to 12 in 1930. But only 12 percent of entering freshmen were finishing. Students in *Who's Who Among Students in American Universities and Colleges* cannot be called a select group—Harvard, Yale, Stanford, and an embarrassing number of other institutions did not participate. The level of our collective taste was not very high: favorite novels were *The Caine Mutiny, The Robe, Gone with the Wind, Magnificent Obsession, The Silver Chalice, The Egyptian, From Here to Eternity, A Man Called Peter,* and *The Old Man and The Sea,* in that order. Farther down the list were *Ethan Frome, The Fountainhead, Look Homeward, Angel, Of Human Bondage,* and *Rebecca*.

James Stewart and June Allyson were the favorite actor and actress, followed by John Wayne, Jane Wyman, Marlon Brando, and Audrey Hepburn. The respondents to the *Who's Who* questionnaire, a select group of brown-nosers, favored classical and symphonic music over all other types, Bing Crosby as performer, and Eddie Fisher among current performers. The editors noted that "a few of the college students choose jive as their favorite kind of music, with Benny Goodman as the favorite performer." Nat King Cole was as advanced as taste got. There was no mention of rhythm and blues or bop.

We preferred suburbia over cities and either over small towns and farms. Teaching was the profession of choice, followed by law, the ministry, and engineering. Those going into business wanted, by a strong majority, to be Organization Men. There were slightly more Democrats than Republicans, almost no independents, and a large number who refused to state a political affiliation.

I like to think that my graduating class at Rockhurst was not typical of this rather dreary group. Certainly we had a higher percentage of entering freshmen graduate in four years—about 35 percent, if the figures from the 1952 yearbook and the commencement list can be trusted. Some of the others had gone into seminaries; some, voluntarily or not, into the armed services; some had just disappeared.

Some of my graduating class even knew what they wanted to do. I may have looked as though I did, especially in the photograph on the Foreword page of the yearbook, exemplifying "a young and modern Rockhurst college, a revitalized, expanding Rockhurst...caught in a moment of immanent activity." At any rate, I had my mouth open and a finger raised. Of course, since I wasn't wearing my glasses, I couldn't see where I was going.

I had come to Rockhurst wanting to be a newspaperman, and despite four years of liberal education and a budding desire to be a writer instead of a reporter, I hadn't figured out a way to become anything else. During much of the second semester of my senior year, I had no idea what to do after graduation and tried not to think about it. I wasn't going to enlist in the army—I wasn't that disoriented. With Knick's encouragement, I sent an application to the University of Kansas graduate program in English in somewhat the same spirit that I now return entries to the Publishers' Clearing House. All year the *Hawk* had carried an ad from Marquette University headed "Continue Your Climb With More EDUCATION," but I had no idea which way was up.

Probably I should have applied for a job at the Kansas City *Star*—Hemingway had worked there; I had grown up with it as the biggest and most important paper imaginable—but instead I searched its want ads looking for reporter's jobs. Only two newspapers, in Iola and Great Bend, both in Kansas, looked promising, or at least possible, and I answered both of them. That was not the kind of movement that *The Snows of Kilimanjaro* had indicated, but it was the best I could manage. Both of them offered me jobs immediately, and it seems clear now that I had underestimated my talents, but at the time I wasn't quite sure what those were. I don't think that Rockhurst had a placement service, and while I may have asked one or two of my teachers to write references, even the laymen were not worldly. Besides, I had somewhere picked up the notion that a newspaperman was supposed to start at the bottom and work his way up, whereas of course in real life what you do is lie like a son of a bitch to get the best job possible and then fake until you can actually do it.

After looking at the map and finding out a little bit about the towns, I chose the job with the Great Bend *Daily Tribune*. It paid 10 percent more—$55 versus $50 a week. Since the Brooklyn *Eagle* closed that year rather than pay $135 to the most experienced members of the newspaper guild, that wasn't bad. But money wasn't the major factor. Great Bend was at least twice as large as Iola, which wasn't any bigger than Boonville, and I didn't want to start *that* small. Iola was in eastern Kansas, which didn't seem all that different from Missouri, and since I was born in Lyons and had relatives in Wichita, I had roots of a sort in west central Kansas.

But Great Bend's real attraction was that it was more than twice as far from Kansas City as Iola. That distance was important for several reasons. For one thing, whatever its shortcomings, Rockhurst hadn't institutionalized me: I knew that my college life was over, and I wanted to put it behind me. The farther I got from Kansas City, the easier that would be because I could not imagine being in Kansas City but not at Rockhurst. For another, I wanted to function independently of my family, and those extra miles would help. Finally, the farther I got from K., the easier it would be to resist her attraction, and Iola formed the apex of a shallow triangle between Kansas City and her hometown.

So I accepted the job in Great Bend and wrote a farewell column for the *Hawk* in my most priggish mode on the theme that college and the adult world have nothing to do with each other because "what you do in college doesn't really count." Apparently I thought that life was real and earnest.

My parents and siblings came to graduation, and perhaps we went to lunch. I don't remember much about the day, but the yearbook has a photo of Dr. Meulemans, the biology teacher, smiling benignly down at my mother and father. I do remember that they brought the first car I owned, purchased on time from my father, who had taken it in trade from a high school classmate of mine. I knew how he treated a car, but that was the deal Dad offered. Anyway, the car—a two-tone gray 1951 Chevrolet six-cylinder two-door—looked sporty, though like all Chevy sixes it topped out at eighty-six miles an hour. It turned out to have no jack in the trunk and very little water in the battery, but this was a case of Dad treating his son as he treated everyone else. I don't think he had checked. He was a terrific salesman, but he was no mechanic.

That night K. and I got back together for a farewell date. The next morning, May 30, 1955, I went to confession to Father

Mac. After he gave me absolution, he warned me that small-town girls would seek to entrap a good-looking, intelligent young man (the first sign of approval I had ever heard from him). Then I packed my clothes, books, and prescription sunglasses I had ordered to wear in the great open spaces, or, as the *Tribune* called it, the Golden Belt Area. I still had the radio, suitcase, electric razor, and, most important—I was going to be a writer—the Royal portable typewriter.

Real Life:

An Anticlimax

It sucks.

—Traditional folk wisdom

In a superficial sense, it was not hard to get settled in Great Bend. After a night or two in a rooming house, I found a clean and comfortable room and bath that a very nice family had just converted from a garage. The husband was a Lennox representative; the wife stayed home; there was a pleasant preteen daughter and a ferocious-looking bulldog that was terrified of moths. If kitchen privileges were included, I didn't use them. I ate breakfast at a restaurant and bakery next door to the *Tribune* office that served odd-tasting coffee and heavily sugared doughnuts. The other two meals I usually caught on the fly between assignments.

The *Tribune* was the largest newspaper between Hutchinson and. . .well, look at a map of Kansas. It was family-owned, and its publisher, whom I rarely saw, was the local representative to the state legislature. Besides wire copy—I never learned to resist looking when the Teletype began to chatter—it reported news from an area bounded by La Crosse, Rush Center, Larned, Hoisington, and Ellinwood with six editorial and news staffers who sat around a cluster of desks in the newsroom and two photographers who lurked in their basement darkroom when not otherwise occupied.

The other staffers were older and more experienced than I, and the only one near my age was married, so I never saw them outside the office. The editor, who had a law degree, was rather short, rather plump, and a little bit gray; his chief assistant was sandy-haired, tall, and thicker in the middle than anywhere else. They must have gotten up to go home or to the bathroom, but in my visual memory, both are rooted to their chairs. The society editor worked part-time in the business office. The sports editor seemed to be about forty and had joined the staff only a few weeks before I came. The chief reporter, also named Bob, was not more than twenty-five and seemed to be the only staff member who acted like my idea of a newspaperman and had the energy and ambition to want to move on.

The photographers might have been hired from central casting. One, called Freddy the Fox, was short and sour and looked rather like the photographer for *Newslife* in *Pogo* whose camera bellows and cigarette drooped at the same angle. The other was younger and more outgoing. Both had worked for Wichita newspapers; both wanted to work for the Denver *Post* or *Rocky Mountain News*; both had a large stock of stories about the newspaper world. They also gave me some elementary instructions about shooting and printing film and tried vainly to teach me to develop it. Keith, the younger photographer, would look dubiously at what I brought back and say, "Well, it's good enough for newsprint." Freddy would just grunt. Neither was married, and they provided what after-hours social life I had in Great Bend.

There wasn't time for much of that. I was hired to do sports and general news, with a little photography on the side, and so I had three jobs on at least two shifts. During the morning I had to be in the newsroom to write stories. During the afternoon I was on call to cover my beat—the firehouse, the less interesting developments at the courthouse, the chamber of commerce and business and farm news, schools (that summer the big stories were defeat of a bond issue in Otis by six votes and ''Poor Color of Wall Block Will Delay Riley Addition''), area news, kiddie birthday parties, what arts there were, and anything else that came up that no one else wanted—and to work on features. Nights and weekends, I covered baseball (the American Legion team; the sports editor took the more important Ban Johnson league games), softball games all over the region (seventeen nights in a row at one stretch), stock car and hot rod races (Great Bend was preparing to host the National Hot Rod Association finals), and at least one rodeo.

In my spare time, I did pieces for the *Herald-Press*, a local weekly that the *Tribune* publisher had acquired. It had a separate office and print shop a few blocks away, and until just before I came a separate editor who had been a town character until he got too colorful. The other Bob—the closest thing to a mentor I had—and I used to speculate about one of us replacing him, but management decided to pay the daily staff a little extra to produce enough to keep it going. After a month or so, Bob showed me how to get hired as a stringer for United Press—he already handled local news for Associated Press.

Mornings were easy enough because, for a while, it was a challenge, working under just enough pressure, to put story after story on material I had just learned about onto the continuous roll of paper fed through my typewriter. The editor made me feel that I was competent at my job. And every day, when we put the paper to bed, I shared with my colleagues a sense of relief and satisfaction that other jobs have never provided.

Getting through the afternoon was difficult because, though the exciting part of the day was over, we had to take a deep breath and go out to get enough material for next day's paper. This got harder for me as the weeks passed.

Partly it was the beat I covered. Potentially the fire station was the most exciting stop, and once, while I was passing through, the bell sounded and the chief yelled to jump aboard the fire engine. But it was a false alarm. I didn't wish anyone hard luck, but even at twenty I would have liked to ride on the engine.

Great Bend wasn't hit by any tornados that summer, but funnels hit all over the area, and the staff would go out hunting for disasters. None of us found any. In my first days on the paper I was left to man the newsroom phones because I didn't know the territory. The National Weather Service reported a funnel at coordinates that meant nothing to me. The big county map on the wall revealed a location just southwest of town. Another time the society editor and one of the photographers went along for the ride when I headed for Dodge City to cover a baseball game. By the time we got to Larned, the sky ahead had turned black and purple, and it was obvious that no game would be played that night. We stopped and called in to see if we needed to cover storm damage in the area, and while I was on the phone, we heard a noise like a train, according to folklore the infallible sign of a tornado. We started to panic until we remembered that we were in the depot and it actually was a train.

A Lower-Middle-Class Education

I never got to cover a fire or a tornado, but I did see enough car accidents to last me. One was particularly bad: a farm truck had pulled out of a side road into the path of a sedan, and the occupants, a family on vacation, had been killed except for one little girl. It was hard to get to the scene because so many people had stopped to watch the bodies being extracted, and my professional voyeur's hatred of the amateur is one thing I retain from my newspaper days.

Fortunately, most of my work was less gruesome. The only thing I can remember doing in the courthouse was getting the list of applicants for marriage licenses. I knew none of the people, and there wasn't even human interest in age disparities, since most of the women listed, in the blank for age, "Consent."

Covering the chamber of commerce took more of my time and got my stories more space, but it did not result in high voltage journalism. In 1955, the big chamber project was to get the designation of U.S. Highway 50 North changed to U.S. 56. This involved endless discussions of how to persuade the other towns on the route to join the campaign by enumerating what seemed to me utterly illusory benefits. Once that was accomplished, there were endless reports filled with mind-numbing, essential details about the paperwork being sent to the federal government. After I left, the petition was granted, and U.S. 56 now stretches from Kansas City through Herington, Dodge City, Montezuma, and Hugoton, Kansas, and Felt, Oklahoma, all the way to Springer, New Mexico. But I never learned how the new avenue of commerce affected these metropoli.

The other big news on that beat was the introduction of Busch Bavarian Beer, which didn't taste as good as Budweiser but was cheaper and probably designed to grab the market share of Falstaff and other down-market beers. If so, that was as successful as the U.S. Highway 56 campaign and far more lucrative.

I did learn that a free lunch was less satisfying than a good story—and also that the effects last about as long and produce pretty much the same results.

Birthday parties were the low point of the day. First I had to group the kids for a photo, with mothers and aunts hovering around like ineffectual sheep dogs. Then I had to take the photo—two photos, to be on the safe side in case someone had a finger up his nose in one shot—and then (this was the hard part), hold them still while I got the names spelled correctly and in the right order. God help you if you made a mistake.

Ordinarily, the *Tribune* wouldn't waste a real photographer on this kind of assignment, but once Freddy and I stopped on the way to a real story, and he took the photo. I wasn't great with kids, but Freddy didn't like anything that moved or talked, and he was looking even grimmer than usual, leaving me the unaccustomed job of being tactful. I thought we were going to have an unseemly incident when an aunt, holding a box brownie in both hands like a squirrel with a nut, asked if she could shoot at the same time as Freddy to use his 1/1000-second strobe light. I thought I was going to have to sit on Freddy.

The feature work was more interesting because it offered more variety. The *Tribune* published an annual special issue on the oil business, and I spent a lot of time bouncing along temporary roads toward rigs where I learned more than I really wanted to know about drilling mud and a whole lot of other technical material that I wrote up and promptly forgot (sort of like my philosophy classes, except that I was getting some fresh air and sunshine—both considered good things in those days— and I got to be in a different place every day).

I was also the resident expert on animal stories: a skunk captured at the concession stand at the softball park; a stray coyote pup who had wandered into town (with photo); a 3½ pound bass that jumped into a boat with a fifteen-inch water

167

snake in its stomach; and an infestation of bats discovered by a cracker salesman and watched by a five-year-old who confided that he could write his name and was going to be a reporter until he became a fireman. I got a by-line for that one.

Another desirable assignment, at least for a while, was photographing and interviewing the candidates for beauty contests in Great Bend and surrounding towns. The Miss Great Bend contest turned into a miniseries. The first queen was also drum majorette of the state champion drum and bugle corps, and the national championships conflicted with the American Royal Queen contest, next rung up on the beauty pageant circuit. She was loyal to the corps. The runner-up was already committed to reigning at the Tri-City Oil Show, which conflicted with the American Royal. Finally a third queen was chosen for the oil show. I don't know who got the luggage, the ten free lessons at the Arthur Murray Dance Studio, and the bouquet, which by that time must have been a little frazzled.

Once, I got to combine beauty and beasts in a feature on a man who crossed greyhounds with staghounds to produce dogs fast enough to catch coyotes and strong enough to fight them. He had a good-looking, halter-top-wearing daughter whom I posed with one of the working dogs and a pet Boston terrier. The girl bent forward just as I tripped the shutter. That was the most successful photo I ever brought back. Freddy and Keith almost took out the darkroom ceiling to raise the enlarger's lens a little higher.

Approval of my newswriting came more quickly. The deskman, whose opinion I respected most, said that I was the best pure writer on the staff. Or perhaps that I was a good writer. If it was the first, I could already see that for myself. If the second, I was either too good or not good enough. My sports clichés were no worse than the sports editor's and my sprightly language no more grating than the area editor's.

Probably it was the first, because I was more interested in writing than I was in news. For one thing, my neck was too long for me to hold the phone receiver between shoulder and ear to take information and type at the same time. This was a serious handicap to a newspaperman. For another, from the editor's point of view, I was interested in the wrong things.

When I covered a stock car race, for example, I noted the winners and point standings, but I was most interested in the men who hadn't placed and probably never would. I wanted to know why they wanted to race and what their lives were like. Even the sports editor, who took a kind of avuncular interest in my career, was not pleased with this story. He ran it, along with an undistinguished photo, but he urged me to concentrate on the winners, the real news.

Perhaps the best thing I wrote in Great Bend didn't appear at all. A few days after the family had been wiped out in the car accident, I drove out to the site between assignments, walked around for a while, and went back to the newsroom to write about the contrast between this normal Kansas day and the numbing sensation of watching emergency crews deal with the wreckage of all those lives ended or irrevocably altered. I tore the piece from the roll of paper, changed a word here and there, and pushed it across to the editor.

After a few minutes, he came around to my desk and stood for a moment. Then he spoke. I can't remember his exact words, but they went something like this: "I'm afraid we can't run this. It's very well done. But the driver of the truck has a lot of relatives in the area. And there may be criminal charges. We don't want to prejudice a jury."

At Rockhurst I had been advised to alter a word here and there, but that had been a game I had played with Knick. This was obviously different, and it's tempting to say that I attained a moral insight into the bankruptcy of small-town journalism, where the implied logo is not the American flag or an eagle but the three monkeys saying, hearing, and seeing no evil. It's also tempting to exaggerate my cynicism and say that I shrugged, rolled up some fresh paper, and started another story.

The truth was probably somewhere in the middle. I could see the editor's point; I could even see that I had written the piece as a way of dealing with all those deaths. Most of the illusions I had about journalism had evaporated. But I had cared about this piece, and at some level I realized that I didn't care about what I was supposed to be doing instead.

It wasn't just U.S. 56 or Busch Bavarian or drilling mud. I had reluctantly given up the dream of being a professional baseball player, but I was still a fan, so it had seemed that sportswriting was an ideal career. In Great Bend, I had gotten to know the kids on the Legion team, liked some of them, wished them well, and sympathized with them when they were eliminated from the regional tournament. But I didn't want to write about them forever, or even their grown-up counterparts. The arms might be stronger, the reflexes faster, but a short to first putout is 6–3 whether it's Peewee Reese to Gil Hodges or Lee Kempf to Bob Hittner. Watching forty different teams on seventeen straight nights must be like having even the best sex with that many partners. I'm not saying that you wouldn't enjoy it, understand, or applaud spectacular moves, but it would be hard to get all that involved emotionally. That, of course, is the secret of any kind of professionalism: to care about the subject but reserve the real passion for the craft. This craft couldn't command my passion. And that was for baseball, which I loved and even understood. As I made the rounds of high school football drills, I dreaded the upcoming season.

Of course, if I had been involved with a person, I might have been less captious about my job. In fact, I didn't have a date the whole time I was in Great Bend. You'd think that covering beauty pageants would be a great way to meet girls, but the obligatory questions and answers were hardly stimulating. I met, casually, some pretty girls in Great Bend, but I didn't ask them out. Partly, I suspect, I was expiating my rejection of K., compared to whom these girls seemed childish; partly I was undergoing a kind of desert fast, though I had no idea what mission I was preparing for. But mostly I was avoiding entanglements with a place I knew I had the talent to leave sooner or later.

My first attempts to write my way up indicated that it might be later. I tried one or two features and sent them to national markets. They had, and deserved, no success. Keith and I worked on a photo feature story that we tried to sell to *Life*, and I learned a good deal, mostly from watching him practice his craft and talk about it, even though the story appeared— on my twenty-first birthday—only in the *Tribune*.

What else did I do? Well, I went to church without ever feeling part of the congregation. Everything else I remember in negation: I don't remember seeing any movies or hearing any live music. Odder still, I don't remember reading any books. I did write about Evan Hunter's novel, *Blackboard Jungle*, in anticipation of the movie's opening in Great Bend, but I had read that in Kansas City. I don't even have a clear memory of where the public library was located. For me, that was far less characteristic than not having dates.

Once, so that I could explain what a major hot rod competition and its crowds were like, the *Tribune* sent Freddy and me to Kansas City to cover a race. Going back was odd because I felt out of place. This was in part physical, for the drag strip was in a part of Kansas City I had never even heard of. In part it was psychological. I stayed at Jim Scott's house, but while we were still friends, we were no longer colleagues and collaborators. I didn't feel that I belonged in Great Bend, but I no longer felt at home in Kansas City.

Most people probably feel this way about their first jobs—Is *this* what it's really about? Why didn't anyone warn me?—so I don't want to be too melodramatic about the desolation of a sensitive, talented youth trapped in a small town. For one thing, that had been done to death by Sherwood Anderson and a host of other writers forty years before I got to Great Bend; for another, most of the time I was too busy to feel sorry for myself. You do one thing; then you do something else; then the day is over and you begin again. And at least I got the recognition of an occasional by-line, and that's a drug that never quite loses its kick.

But working at the wrong job is like hitting yourself on the head or living in a bad marriage. You can do it, but it feels good when you stop. Late that summer the University of Kansas admitted me to the M.A. program and offered me a teaching assistantship. Jim Scott had already been accepted. I had no idea what graduate school involved, and the assistantship paid even worse than the *Tribune*, but the opportunity was irresistible for two reasons: it got me out of Great Bend, and it would pay me to read books and talk about them.

As soon as I got the offer, I gave notice to the publisher. He seemed startled. Was it the money? He could improve that. I was pleased to hear that I had been worth my keep and more, but I told him that I was going to try something else. A few months later, when my morale as a new graduate student was exceptionally low, the other Bob called to urge me to apply for the job of sports editor on a much larger morning paper he had recently joined. He assured me that I could get it.

I was discouraged, but I turned him down for two reasons: it was in K.'s hometown, and I had just read Grantland Rice's autobiography. Most people have probably never heard of Grantland Rice, which represents some progress. He was the founder of modern sportswriting and its most famous practitioner until he died in 1954. He wrote his book from the pinnacle of success in a mood of complete self-satisfaction. And as I read the book, I could only think, "What an awful way to spend your life." Nearly forty years later, seeing what years on the sports page have done to Jim Murray's brain, I am satisfied with my choice.

In fact, it wasn't a choice because Rockhurst had spoiled me for the newspaper business. Four hundred years of Jesuit education didn't have that specifically in mind, but I'm grateful anyway.

Aftermath

Jim Scott and I returned to Rockhurst once or twice from Lawrence for brief visits to Knick. But when, in 1957, I left the Kansas City area, I did not return to the campus for more than twenty-five years. Reunions didn't interest me because I hadn't wanted to talk to many of my classmates in 1955 and I suspected that time had probably not improved them. Jim stayed in closer touch and reported that, from my point of view, I was right. The quarter of the arts and sciences graduates who went on to get doctorates were scattered across the country.

I knew what had happened to my real teachers, but most of them had moved on, too. Father O'Sullivan had been transferred to Regis College in Denver years before—I had sent him offprints of some early articles on Evelyn Waugh. A year or so after I graduated, the dullest teacher I encountered in twenty years in the classroom resented Father McCallin's influence and had confronted the president with the ultimatum that he or Father Mac would have to go. Somewhere I heard that the one exception to the Jesuit vow of obedience concerned women: no Jesuit was obliged to teach them. I don't know that this was true, though it sounded plausible, but when Father Mac was assigned to St. Louis University, which had a graduate program and was also coed, he went. I was told that he was not happy there, though women may have had nothing to do with that.

I tried to stay in touch with him until, after some years as a teacher myself, I realized that he was more important to me than the other way round. He was the first person I saw when I arrived at Rockhurst and the last when I left, and the loss of that connection broke already attenuated ties to Rockhurst. To me it meant people rather than a place, and the people were gone.

Once I drove by the campus with my older daughter on the way to visit her grandfather and cousins in Boonville. She had just been subjected to the grand tour of scenes from her mother's youth and announced, with teenage hauteur and boredom, "I never want to see anyplace that either of my parents has ever been!"

I didn't press the issue, since by that time Rockhurst and I had changed considerably. In 1969, women were admitted in the daytime. (The College of Saint Teresa, which had changed its name to Avila and moved to far southern Kansas City in 1963, went coed at the same time as Rockhurst.)

From the point of view of an arts snob, worse was to follow: Rockhurst started an M.B.A. program, and in 1983, as the current catalog puts it, "initiated the establishment of a School of Management consolidating the existing business programs. Nonbusiness programs are housed in the College of Arts and Sciences." Student nurses and physical and occupational therapists came on board.

Vatican II and New Age philosophy had their effects even on the Jesuits, who in any case formed a smaller percentage of the faculty than they had in my day. A catalog from that period asserts confidently, if rather dryly, that

> Rockhurst is a Catholic liberal arts college which provides those means that are considered best to form the cultured Christian gentleman. It lays a foundation in learning and culture, which later may be followed, if desired, by specialized courses in the professional schools, and provides experience designed to help the student to train his will and to control his emotions. It seeks to produce the educated man possessed of a mind trained to orderly thinking, broad knowledge and understanding, social competency, and a practical Christian philosophy of living—in short, to build an integrated personality.

The current philosophy looks outward rather than inward, and the language is far moister. "Community" is used in two of four statements in "Our Mission Today." It shows up in all four under "Foundations for a College of Excellence" as "A caring community," "A community of purpose," "A just community," and "A diverse community." To adapt Dwight MacDonald's line about *Our Town*, I agree with everything the catalog says, but I will fight to the death the right to say it that way. Partly this is due to the old grad's desire to have everything stay the same; partly it is due to a preference for the language of my period.

I wasn't aware of the new rhetoric until I began writing this book, but having taught at a Jesuit university and four state-supported universities by then, I had lost most of my illusions about education. I did know that the rhetoric of liberal education had become so stale that not even administrators were using it much any more. Rockhurst had become, like Boonville, part of the past that I thought I had outgrown. When people asked about my undergraduate college, I said that, since it was now full of women and business majors, it had no further interest for me.

But after thirty years as a scholar, I began to think about the past and what it meant to me—first Boonville and then, after a hiatus, Rockhurst. I dug out my transcript, my senior yearbook, and my copies of the *Hawk*; I began to recall the texture of those years: names, faces, incidents, courses, conversations. I wrote to Bob Knickerbocker. Finally I returned to the campus, forty-one years after I first arrived.

The student body and the number of buildings had more than doubled. There were real dormitories, a separate student union, a new library, even a fraternity house, which didn't look much more substantial than the old barracks.

Father Freeman was still teaching, and a chair in Philosophy had been named after him. When I inquired about the location of the archives, I was told that I would have to see Father Gough. Even after forty years, that was a shock, but when I found him in the basement of the Greenlease Library, I discovered that either I had toughened or he had mellowed. He seemed smaller than he had in 1951, but in fact he had changed far less than I, his hair as white and thick as when I first saw him. We had a pleasant conversation about the old days and his one trip to Boonville to give a retreat; he pressed on me duplicate copies of the yearbook in order to clear shelf space; and he said, as I left, "God bless."

Bob Knickerbocker had retired, first as moderator of the *Hawk* after thirty years and then from teaching, but still came in to counsel students in the Learning Center when he wasn't visiting his numerous grandchildren or traveling purely for pleasure. He remembered me—and every other *Hawk* editor—

quite well, but he was surprised to learn that I was only thirteen years his junior and took more pills than he did.

The college has changed. Tuition, $175 a semester in my day, is now $4,000, and my social and financial peers have given way to affluent and full-need students at either end of the scale. The dormitories that replaced the barracks are in turn being replaced by town houses because students refuse to live in corridor dormitories, where the lowest common denominator prevails. Some things have not changed.

I met the current creative writing teacher, who is shorter and darker than Father O'Sullivan, and the dean of the arts faculty, who is taller and heartier than Father Gough. They seemed amused at my quotations of the more sexist parts of the recruiting brochure. This was generous, since both are women.

Father McCallin did not live to see this. The brother of the man who married K. said his funeral mass. The irony seemed torturous but fitting.

I finished a Ph.D. in English and became a professor. But that, as Kipling used to say, is another story.